KAPLAN pmbr

FINALS

REMEDIES

CORE CONCEPTS AND KEY QUESTIONS

Second Edition

T. Leigh Hearn
Series Editor

Published by Kaplan Publishing, a division of Kaplan, Inc.
1 Liberty Plaza, 24th floor
New York, NY 10006

Printed in the United States of America

10 9 8 7 6 5 4 3 2 1

ISBN13: 978-1-60714-100-6

TABLE OF CONTENTS

I. REQUIREMENTS FOR EQUITABLE REMEDIES

A. JURISDICTIONAL BASIS

1. **In General:** Under the merged system of law and equity, a court of general jurisdiction may render an equitable decree as long as the traditional jurisdictional prerequisites are met.

   a. **Actions *in personam*:** For actions in personam, there must be jurisdiction over the subject matter and jurisdiction over the person (namely, the defendant).

   b. **Actions *in rem*:** For actions *in rem* (or *quasi in rem*) there must be jurisdiction over the subject matter and the *res* (the thing or property) in dispute.

2. **Equitable Jurisdiction:** Assuming an equity court has such primary jurisdiction, the next question is whether equitable jurisdiction exists. This simply means whether the dispute is one that is traditionally cognizable in equity.

3. **Situations Involving Equitable Jurisdiction:** As a general rule, equitable jurisdiction exists in the following cases:

   a. **No adequate remedy at law:** The traditional view is that before granting equitable relief, the court must find the absence of an adequate legal remedy; *or*

   b. **Actions in which equity developed the substantive law:** There are certain types of action where the remedy has been traditionally equitable in nature (e.g., trusts, divorce, matters relating to fiduciary obligations).

4. **Inadequacy of Legal Remedy:** There is no one formula for determining when a legal remedy is inadequate. However, there are some common patterns where the equitable remedy is usually granted. Courts may seek to determine if the legal remedy is complete, practical, and efficient. Other courts may focus on whether there is a substantial injury for which there is no legal remedy. Here are some illustrations:

   a. The plaintiff is deprived of some thing to which she is entitled, because the defendant has committed a tort or a breach of contract. The legal remedy of damages will not do because she needs the thing itself. Thus, the plaintiff will get equitable relief by way of injunction or specific performance.

      Example: Specific performance of an option contract to purchase stock was granted on a showing that the stock was not traded on the market and was seldom exchanged [*Chadwell v. English*, 652 P.2d 310 (Okla. 1982)].

      Example: Plaintiff, owner of a tomato factory, sues to force defendant-tomato grower to deliver the tomatoes promised in a contract. Although the market value of the promised crop is easily calculable, the unavailability of tomatoes from other sources means that plaintiff necessarily would default on some of its obligations to supply others and would suffer an irreparable loss of reputation thereby. Under these circumstances, specific performance may be appropriate as the legal remedy clearly is inadequate. [*Curlice Bros. v. Catts*, 66 A. 935 (NJ, 1907)].

b. The defendant acts in such a way that the plaintiff may be required to bring more than one suit to effectuate her legal remedy. This is a hardship, and equity may avoid it by awarding more adequate relief.

   Example: If the defendant repeatedly trespasses on the plaintiff's land, equity may enjoin the trespass rather than force repeated actions at law to redress the injury.

c. The plaintiff is entitled either to money or certain performance by the defendant. Money, recoverable at law, would be an entirely adequate remedy, but the defendant is insolvent and it is not collectable. However, the defendant is still capable of rendering the performance to which the plaintiff is entitled as an alternative to the money. Under the circumstances, equity may order performance.

d. The plaintiff is entitled to damages at law, and this would be adequate if damages could be measured with any reasonable degree of accuracy, but, under the facts, damages are so speculative that any award is likely to be inadequate.

5. **Inadequacy Not Enough:** The mere inadequacy or lack of a legal remedy does not, *ipso facto*, establish an absolute right to equitable relief; it only allows the claimant to request it. Relief continues, however, to be largely a matter of judicial discretion. For example, an employer may ask the court to specifically enforce an employment contract, arguing that a legal remedy (i.e., damages) is not adequate because the employee has unique skills. Nonetheless, employment contracts are not specifically enforceable based partly on the difficulty of supervising enforcement of the decree and partly on the undesirability of imposing an employment relationship on persons who are in serious disagreement.

II. INJUNCTIVE RELIEF

A. TYPES OF INJUNCTIONS

1. **Mandatory Injunction.** A mandatory injunction is one that requires the defendant to perform an affirmative act and is enforceable by the contempt power of the court.

   Example: Plaintiff, a 30-year-old male, brings an action against Health Club, an all-women's health facility, to allow him to take aerobics classes there. If the court requires the health club to admit him, it will do so in the form of a mandatory injunction.

Example: Plaintiff, a real estate developer, brings an action against City to allow him to build a new hotel on the City's waterfront. If the court requires City to allow the hotel construction, it will do so in the form of a mandatory injunction.

2. **Prohibitory Injunction.** A prohibitory injunction is one that forbids the defendant from acting.

   Example: Plaintiff, a small publishing company, brings an action against defendant, a large publishing company, to keep it from publishing a magazine conceptualized and developed by plaintiff. If the court rules in plaintiff's favor, it will issue a prohibitory injunction.

   Example: Plaintiff, a women's health clinic, brings an action against defendant, an antiabortion group, to enjoin it from harassing protesters on the sidewalk in front of the clinic. If the court so enjoins the defendant, it will do so in the form of a prohibitory injunction.

3. **Temporary Restraining Order (TRO) vs. Preliminary Injunction.** Temporary injunctive relief, which can take the form of a temporary restraining order or a preliminary injunction, can perform the valuable task of preserving the status quo while the judicial proceedings are pending.

   a. **Temporary restraining orders.** A TRO may be issued to forestall the occurrence of ***imminent irreparable harm*** pending a hearing for a preliminary injunction.

      i. **Ex parte orders.** A TRO may be granted *ex parte*, i.e., on affidavits of the complainant without affording the defendant notice or an opportunity to be heard. The plaintiff must, however, make a strong showing as to why such notice and hearing should not be required.

         (a) **Duration.** As a general rule, a TRO is limited to a period of about ten days.

         (b) **Time to take effect.** A TRO does not take effect until the defendant has been notified of its existence.

         (c) **Review by the court.** When a TRO has been issued *ex parte*, upon receiving notice of the order the defendant may request its immediate review.

         (d) **Stays of TROs.** When a defendant requests review of a prohibitory injunction, that injunction is generally not stayed. Mandatory injunctions, however, are generally stayed pending review when so requested by a defendant.

   b. **Preliminary injunctions.** A preliminary injunction (sometimes referred to as a temporary injunction or interlocutory injunction) is distinguishable from

Type of injunction	*Characteristics*	*Duration*	*Available ex parte?*
Mandatory	Requires the defendant to perform an affirmative act.	May be temporary or permanent.	Yes, but difficult to get *ex parte* as it requires an affirmative act on defendant's part.
Prohibitory	Forbids the defendant from continuing to act in a certain way.	May be temporary or permanent.	Yes, but does not take effect until defendant has actual notice of order.
TRO	Issued to forestall the occurrence of an imminent, irreparable harm pending a hearing for a preliminary injunction. Usually prohibitory in nature, but may be mandatory.	Usually no more than ten days, or until defendant is able to be heard, whichever comes first.	Yes, but plaintiff must make a strong showing as to why notice and a hearing should not be required. (i.e., to avoid evasive action by the defendant.)
Preliminary	Usually used to preserve the status quo until a more formal hearing may be held. Usually prohibitory in nature, but may be mandatory.	Until a final hearing on the matter may be held.	No.
Permanent	Permanently requires or forbids some action on the part of the defendant.	Until such time as circumstances change and the parties petition the court for a change in the order.	No.

a TRO in that it is of longer duration and is issued only ***after notice and an adversary hearing***. An ***injunctive bond*** is usually required in the event that the moving party loses the action for permanent injunction and the preliminary injunction causes injury to the enjoined party.

4. **Permanent injunction.** A permanent injunction is intended by the court to be in effect permanently. This does not mean that future circumstances can not cause the court to reverse its decision.

B. INADEQUACY OF LEGAL REMEDY

1. **In General:** A court will enjoin a person from certain conduct or order her to undertake affirmative conduct only when it has been demonstrated that her action or failure to act would cause harm for which there is no adequate legal remedy.

   a. **Grounds for inadequacy:** There are four categories of legal inadequacy that may be sufficient to permit the court to consider issuing injunctive relief:

      i. **Multiplicity of litigation:** Inadequacy may be found if the plaintiff would need to bring multiple or sequential lawsuits in order to take advantage of the legal remedy.

      Example: Equity will enjoin continuing trespasses or blocking of an alley. A good illustration of a continuing trespass occurs when debris is dumped on the plaintiff's land. At least where the plaintiff cannot easily remove the debris herself, courts will issue a mandatory injunction to compel its removal and/or a prohibitory injunction to prohibit further dumping.

      ii. **Difficulty in measuring damages:** When there are significant problems in measuring the damages (i.e., the existence or amount of money damages is speculative or conjectural), the legal remedy may be deemed inadequate.

      iii. **The injury being caused to plaintiff is irreparable:** In many circumstances, damages, though calculable, will not provide an adequate substitute for the loss or harm suffered by the plaintiff.

      Example: Toxic fumes from a factory has the effect of destroying trees, crops, and other vegetation on plaintiff's farm.

      Exam tip: In the case of nuisances, the injunctive remedy in equity is almost always superior to the money remedy at law. The plaintiff in such cases has suffered diminished use and enjoyment of her own land, and, unless it is purely commercial land, it cannot be fully compensated for in money. Thus, in such cases, injunctions are granted willingly where the only issue is adequacy of legal remedy, though they may be denied when factors of hardship or public interest are weighed in the balance.

      iv. **Willful nature of defendant's conduct:** Quite often the defendant's willful or malicious misconduct will make it appropriate to give plaintiff the remedy of her choice.

         (a) **Protection of privacy rights:** Although earlier decisions declined to grant injunctive relief in privacy cases, such reasoning today is rejected outright by practically all courts.

Example: Injunction granted to prevent rejected suitor from continuing to harass plaintiff. [*Kramer v. Douvey*, 680 S.W.2d. 524 (Tex., 1984)].

b. **Test for appropriateness of an injunction.** An injunction is considered appropriate when the remedy at law is inadequate (see above), when the injunction is enforceable, and when the benefit to plaintiff outweighs the hardship to defendant.

i. **Enforceability of the decree.** Naturally, the court does not want to issue an order that would prove difficult or impossible to enforce. Note that this is generally more of a problem with mandatory injunctions, where the defendant must do an affirmative act that the court must supervise, than with prohibitory injunctions, where the court can simply sanction the defendant for continuing the disallowed activity.

ii. **Balancing of the hardships.** Where the hardship to the defendant outweighs the benefit of the injunction to the plaintiff, plaintiff's motion for injunction will generally be denied.

Example: Defendant builds a very expensive boathouse. The boathouse is mostly on his own property, but, after construction is complete, plaintiff discovers that it encroaches 25 feet onto plaintiff's property. When plaintiff brings this to defendant's attention, defendant is horrified, as he did not know that he was encroaching on plaintiff's land. Plaintiff brings a motion for a mandatory injunction ordering defendant to remove the boathouse from his property. Judgment for defendant is likely, as tearing down the boathouse will be considered more of a hardship to defendant than benefit to plaintiff. Note that plaintiff may be able to claim (and win) monetary damages in this situation.

C. NATURE OF INTERESTS PROTECTIBLE IN EQUITY

1. **Unique Chattels:** A mandatory injunction ordering defendant to return a converted chattel is granted where the remedy at law (replevin or damages) is not adequate. To establish the inadequacy of the remedy at law, it must shown that the chattel wrongfully taken is "unique."

a. **Nature of uniqueness:** While uniqueness is variously defined, the underlying principle is that the chattel cannot be replaced through the market. Included within this definition are articles that quite literally are "one of a kind" (e.g., a rare Inca artifact or document signed by George Washington). Also, note that the uniqueness of an item may be based upon ***sentimental value*** (as in the case of a family heirloom or wedding ring).

Example: Thief, Susie's brother, converts Susie's engagement ring and gives it to his girlfriend. Susie asks Thief to return the ring, but he refuses. Susie brings an action against Thief to require him to return the ring. Because the ring is unique (Susie's husband designed it himself), and because it has great sentimental value, a mandatory injunction is appropriate in this instance.

2. **Land Damage:** Since land is always considered to be unique and thus damage to it is viewed as irreparable, ***trespass, nuisance,*** and ***equitable waste*** involving any interest in real property will be enjoined if:

   a. **Continuous nature of the wrongful act:** The tortious conduct is of a continuing nature so as to make legal relief overly burdensome or uneconomical to the parties and/or the courts; or

   b. **Imminent injury:** The threatened or imminent tortious destruction or injury to realty will result in irreparable harm for which money damages will be inadequate.

   Example: A life tenant "without impeachment for waste" is in possession of Blackacre on which a ten-story apartment building is located. The life tenant proposes to raze the apartment building so that she can build a single-story dwelling on the same site. This is an example of equitable waste that can be enjoined by either the reversioner or remainderman.

   Example: John, who leases Whiteacre, chops down many trees on the property for firewood and lumber, both of which he sells to stores and suppliers for his own profit. To date, he has cleared more than an acre. He has been chopping trees down for several months, and, when so requested by the landlord, refuses to stop. The court will probably enjoin him from cutting down any more trees.

   Example: Sarah, who lives next door to Blueacre, picks walnuts and apples off Blueacre's trees without permission. The owner has asked her to stop, but she continues to do so. While the court will probably enjoin her from continuing to pick the nuts and fruits, the owner is also probably entitled to money damages, which may be easily quantifiable in this case (as they are capable of reproduction).

3. **Non-possessory Interests in Land:** Equity will protect such non-possessory or incorporeal interests in land such as easements, profits and equitable servitudes.

   a. **Remedy at law inadequate:** The law views property as unique. No two parcels of land are ever regarded as the same. Likewise, incorporeal (non-possessory) interests in land such as easements and profits are also considered to be unique.

   b. **Injunctions:** Whenever there is unreasonable or substantial interference with the exercise of such property rights (e.g., by placing a barrier across a roadway over which plaintiff has an easement or preventing a profit-holder from entering land to remove minerals or some substance therefrom), the damage is deemed irreparable. Thus, injunctive relief is granted because of the inadequacy of the remedy at law.

Example: Tricia has an easement across Blackacre for ingress and egress. Without using a driveway that cuts across Blackacre, she cannot reach the road from her house, which is landlocked. John, who owns Blackacre, is annoyed at Tricia for stirring up dust when she goes down the driveway, so he erects an electric fence across the driveway. Tricia is entitled to a mandatory injunction requiring John to remove the fence and allow her to use the driveway.

Example: Zoe holds a profit that allows her to pick blueberries on Blueberryacre. Steve, the owner, feels that Zoe has been taking too many berries, so he places a stun gun near the berries that is set to shoot Zoe whenever she approaches them. Zoe is entitled to a mandatory injunction requiring Steve to remove the stun gun and allow her to pick berries.

i. **Easement must be recognized at law:** Before relief can be granted in equity, there must be a legally protected right. Thus, for example, where easements of light and air are not recognized at law, no protection will be granted.

Example: Defendant constructed an addition to his hotel that blocked out the sun on the beach in front of plaintiff's hotel. Equity courts refused to grant injunctive relief because applicable state laws did not recognize easements for light and air. [*Fontainebleau Hotel Corp. v. Forty-Five Twenty-Five, Inc.*, 114 So.2d 357 (Fla., 1959)].

Example: Defendant owns a waterfront home. Plaintiff, defendant's neighbor to the rear (away from the water), brings an action for injunction against defendant to prevent him from building a third story on his home that would block plaintiff's view of the water. The court will not enjoin defendant unless a negative easement for a view exists in this jurisdiction (which it does not in most).

4. **Real Property Interests-Injunctive Relief Denied:** There are certain situations involving real property interests in which equitable relief may be denied.

a. **Encroachment:** Where, by mistake or inadvertence, a building or other structure is constructed in such a way as to encroach upon plaintiff's property, a claim for trespass arises. The equity court, however, may refuse to order destruction or modification of the encroaching building because of the relative hardship to the defendant.

i. **Balance of hardships defense:** Under such circumstances, the defendant's cost of removal of the encroachment may far exceed the value of the land restored to the plaintiff. Thus, courts will generally "balance the hardships" in determining whether injunctive relief should be granted.

(a) **Intentional or deliberate encroachment:** It is important to note that such a "balancing" test applies only in situations involving inadvertent encroachment. On the other hand, whenever defendant's conduct is intentional or deliberate, an injunction may be issued regardless of the hardships on defendant.

Example: Defendant knowingly built a home encroaching on power company's easement. The court held that defendant's conduct was deliberate and ordered him to remove the $16,000 home from the encroached property. [*Missouri Power & Light Comp. v. Barnett*, 354 S.W.2d 873 (Mo., 1962)].

b. **Simple acts of trespass:** For simple acts of trespass causing no injury to the realty (e.g., throwing an object on plaintiff's property), the landowner usually has a cause of action for at least ***nominal*** damages.

i. **Exception:** Where the trespass is repetitive and constitutes an ongoing interference or invasion with plaintiff's right of exclusive possession, injunctive relief may be available.

Example: An injunction was properly granted to prohibit golf balls from being propelled onto plaintiff's property from a neighboring golf course. [*Fenton v. Quaboag Country Club*, 333 N.E.2d 216 (Mass., 1967)].

c. **Industrial nuisance:** Equitable relief may be denied in nuisance cases if such relief might operate inequitably against plaintiff's business or enterprise. This is frequently the case where a plaintiff and owner seeks an injunction which, if granted, would result in shutting down a useful and costly enterprise.

i. **Balance of hardships doctrine:** In such situations, most courts will "balance the hardships" so that if the economic consequences to defendant ***greatly outweigh*** the interference with plaintiff's property rights, the injunction may be denied. In this case, the plaintiff may obtain recovery for damages only.

Example: Court refused to enjoin operation of manure processing plant, citing loss of jobs and loss of a useful product as primary factors to be taken into account in the balancing process. [See *Padilla v. Lawrence*, 685 R.2d 964 (N. Mex., 1984)].

d. **Public nuisance:** A public nuisance covers any disturbance that endangers the public health, safety, and welfare (e.g., a house of prostitution or gambling facility).

i. **Remedy:** As a general rule, equity courts will ***not*** act to enjoin crimes. Thus, where the public nuisance involves criminal activity, equitable relief will not be granted unless a criminal prosecution would constitute an inadequate remedy.

ii. **Alternative relief:** Quite often the court will frame its decree to allow the continuation of a productive business or industry by ***ordering the defendant to mitigate*** the nuisance to the extent scientifically possible (e.g., installing filters on drains causing the pollution of a river).

(a) **Compromise injunctions:** In some cases, the equity court will grant partial relief, such as limiting the burning of waste to certain hours or restricting airplanes from flying over certain populated areas.

5. **Equity Will Restrain Waste:** Equity will restrain waste that causes an unjustifiable diminution of a future interest in property if the legal remedy proves inadequate.

a. **Voluntary waste:** Voluntary waste consists of deliberate destructive acts done by one rightfully in possession of the land (e.g., tenant).

i. **Damages:** Damages are measured either by the diminution in value (i.e., the difference in value of the property before and after the injury) or by the cost of repairs.

ii. **Injunctive relief:** Equitable relief is also available where the remedy at law is inadequate. Since by definition such waste results in permanent injury to the freehold (e.g., the destruction of a forest), money damages cannot compensate for such loss. Consequently, a prohibitory injunction ordering the defendant to desist from the destructive acts is granted.

b. **Permissive waste:** Affirmative voluntary waste should be distinguished from permissive waste in which inaction results in damage (e.g., failure of tenant to repair a leaky roof causing damage to floors). Generally, this type of waste consists of failure to keep premises in proper repair.

i. **Remedy:** Usually damages are the appropriate remedy as measured by the cost of repairs.

c. **Ameliorating waste:** Ameliorating waste consists of acts done by the tenant that alter the freehold but which results in a beneficial change that ***increases the value of the property*** (e.g., modification of buildings or the construction of improvements).

i. **Remedy:** Ordinarily, no damages can be recovered because there is ***no diminution*** in the value of the property. Likewise, equitable relief is seldom granted since it is not possible to show irreparable injury.

d. **Equitable waste:** Equitable waste consists of material changes in the freehold by a person lawfully in possession (e.g., life tenant) who is not chargeable with voluntary waste. Typically, this arises where a life tenant "without impeachment for waste" engages in destructive acts (e.g., life tenant desires to demolish dwelling house so that he can build a tennis court).

i. **Injunctive relief:** Since the person in possession is not chargeable with legal waste, injunctive relief is the only appropriate remedy available. Thus, the remainderman or reversioner may protect his beneficial interest by enjoining such destructive acts.

6. **Intangible Property Interests:** Equity will protect intangible property interests that have economic value. The rationale for granting relief in these contexts typically is that damages at law would be measured by lost profits and thus would be conjectural and difficult to prove. Moreover, the defendant's wrongful conduct is generally recurring so that plaintiff would have to engage in multiple or continuous actions to protect his rights.

a. **Types of interests protected:**

i. **Fair competition:** A variety of different practices have been held to be unfair competition and to threaten the plaintiff with irreparable harm.

(a) **Trade libel:** A trade libel may be defined as a statement disparaging the plaintiff's business, product, or services for the purpose of persuading or inducing customers or the public not to do business with the plaintiff.

(1) **Relief:** In certain cases trade libel may be enjoined (e.g., where it occurs in conjunction with another enjoinable tort such as unfair competition or trademark infringement), but courts are hesitant to grant equitable relief because of the constitutional guarantees of freedom of speech and jury trial.

ii. **Inducing breach of contract**

(a) **Damages:** Most courts apply a tort measure of damages permitting the plaintiff to recover for all injuries proximately caused by the contract-breaker.

(b) **Injunctive relief:** An injunction is rarely granted against a third-party tortfeasor who interferes with an existing contract mainly because the cause of action arises ***after*** the breach. As a consequence, if the wrong has already been completed, then plaintiff's only remedy is for damages.

iii. **Patents, copyrights, trademarks:** Patents, copyrights, and trademarks are thought to be ***unique intangibles***, and infringement by competitors or misuse by licensees will generally be enjoined upon presentation of adequate proof.

(a) **Damages:** The copyright statute (17 USC 504) also sets forth two different methods of calculating damages to an injured copyright holder:

(1) Actual damages suffered plus any profits of the infringer that are attributable to the infringement and not taken into account in computing the actual damages; or

(2) Statutory damages.

iv. **Trade names, unfair competition (palming off):** A business will be protected from a competitor who seeks to benefit from an established trade name by a similar or identical name. The "key" determination is whether the trade name actually has acquired a reputation as the name designating certain goods. The fact that the plaintiff used a particular name before the defendant's use is not sufficient in and of itself to require relief. The important question is whether X is ***"palming off"*** his or her products as the products of Y.

Example: In a case involving a related type of unfair competition (namely, the use of titles), a California court held that the national distributor of the French film, "The Story of O" could not compel defendant-producer of "The Journey of O" to change its title (i.e., no mandatory injunction) but could require him to take steps to dispel the likelihood of confusion by including disclaimers. [*Allied Artists Pictures Corp. v. Friedman*, 68 Cal. App. 3d 127 (1977)].

Example: Use of the name "California Western" by a university caused public confusion and irreparable harm to the law school with the same name. [*California Western School of Law v. California Western University* 125 Cal. App. 3d 1002 (1981)].

Compare: Use of the initials PMBE to describe its Preliminary Multistate Bar Examination held ***not likely to cause confusion*** among bar applicants into thinking that defendant's exam had any official connection with the actual MBE. [*National Conference of Bar Examiners and Educational Testing Service v. Multistate Legal Studies, Inc.*, 692 E.2d 478 (7th Cir., 1982)].

v. **Trade secrets:** Persons who have established a confidential or fiduciary relationship (as is often the case in employment relations) may be enjoined from using trade secrets for their own benefit. Equitable jurisdiction is based on the inadequacy of damages where (a) the secret

PROPERTY INTERESTS–AVAILABLE REMEDIES FOR INTERFERENCE			
Type of property/situation	***Injunction available?***	***Damages available?***	***Special rules***
Unique personal property	Yes.	Possibly, if deprivation of chattel caused some kind of economic loss.	Chattel must be genuinely one-of-a-kind or hold great sentimental value.
Personal property that is not unique	No.	Yes, as money damages will compensate plaintiff for his loss.	Note that criminal actions may also be appropriate.
Land damage	Yes, because land is always considered to be unique and the damage to it irreparable.	Possibly.	For an injunction, legal relief must be overly burdensome or imminent, irreparable injury must be present.
Interference with non-possessory interests in land	Yes, because incorporeal interests in land are considered to be unique.	Not usually, unless in addition to future harm the plaintiff can prove past economic harm.	Note that the interest must be recognized at law.
Encroachment	No, if encroachment is by mistake or if it would be a hardship to the defendant.	Yes, if plaintiff can prove actual loss in property/ resale value or other economic harm.	If encroachment is deliberate, then injunction is appropriate, even if it poses a hardship to the defendant.
Trespass	Yes, if there are actual damages or if it is repetitive and constitutes an ongoing interference. Otherwise, no.	Yes, if it is a simple trespass causing no injury to the land, nominal damages are available.	Analyze the frequency of the trespass and damage to the land.
Industrial nuisance	No, if the economic consequences to defendant greatly outweigh interference with plaintiff's property rights.	Yes, if injunction is not available or if injunction is for future restraint and plaintiff demonstrates past economic harm.	Balancing of the hardships is key.
Public nuisance	Partial relief may be available, but not for criminal activity.	Probably not.	Covers any disturbance that threatens public health, safety and welfare.
Voluntary waste	Yes, in the form of a prohibitory injunction.	Yes, measured by the diminution in value or by the cost of repairs.	Note that damages and injunctive relief are not mutually exclusive!
Permissive waste	No.	Yes, as measured by the cost of repairs.	Where inaction results in damage.
Ameliorating	No, because there is no irreparable injury.	No, because there is benefit to the owner.	You only get remedies where there has been injury or harm!
Intangible property interests	Yes, because damages would be difficult to prove and because of multiplicity of litigation.	Not usually, as they are too hard to prove. Compensatory damages are available in some instances where they are provable.	

is unique or (b) the secret is disclosed in confidence by employer to employee.

(a) **Damages as remedy:** Any tortious appropriation or disclosure of a trade secret constitutes a misappropriation of plaintiff's "property" interest. Usually the plaintiff is entitled to recover ***compensatory damages*** measured by the profits that the defendant reaped from his tortious act or the plaintiff's lost profits.

vi. **Customer list cases:** A special type of problem dealing with trade secrets involves the so-called "customer list" or "route" cases. Quite often, a rival employer will hire away a salesperson who made the customer contacts or developed the route. In such cases, injunctive relief is generally limited to solicitation of former customers, but not the acceptance of patronage from them.

(a) **Agreements not to disclose specifically enforced:** Modernly, employers frequently require their employees to sign agreements not to make any unauthorized disclosure of trade secrets to which they may become privy during the course of their employment. Such contracts are generally valid and specifically enforceable.

D. PROTECTION OF NON-PROPRIETARY RIGHTS

1. **In General:** Equity traditionally did not protect personal rights (as opposed to property rights). Today, however, such reasoning is rejected outright by most courts. The availability of equitable relief now turns upon the adequacy of legal damages. Nonetheless, without the threat to a property right, equity generally will ***not*** be available to restrain the following:

   a. **Threatened assault and battery:** Since this is a matter related to criminal law, equitable relief is not an appropriate means by which to enjoin a threatened assault or battery.

   b. **Domestic relations cases:** Equity generally has denied injunctive relief in domestic relations cases in which a husband or wife has sought the aid of the court to restrain a spouse's alleged immoral conduct. As the court stated in *Lyon v. Izen*, 268 N. E. 2d 436 (M., 1971), "the difficulty, if not impossibility of enforcement, and the very doubtful beneficial results to be obtained thereby, warrant the denial of such a decree." In brief, most courts are unanimous in their belief that the problem of extramarital conduct cannot be resolved by the use of injunctions.

   c. **Right to privacy:** The availability of equitable relief now turns upon the adequacy of legal damages. If a tortious invasion has in fact been completed, then money damages may be assessed to compensate the injured party. Where proof supports a finding of malice in the sense of personal ill will or reckless disregard of plaintiff's rights, punitive damages may even be recovered. If the invasion is a continuing one, however, injunctive relief is the most practical and effective remedy.

Example: Defendant, a freelance photographer, kept plaintiffs Jackie Onassis and her family under constant surveillance, following them everywhere they went and snapping photographs in their faces. Injunctive relief was granted to prevent the continuing invasions of their privacy. The defendant was ordered to approach no closer than twenty-five feet from Jackie and thirty feet from her children, and to desist "shadowing" them. [*Galella v. Onassis*, 487 F.2d 986 (2d Cir., 1973)].

d. **Threatened or actual defamation of character:** Defamation is thought to be so interwoven with the free speech guarantee of the First Amendment that prior restraints are abjured and a jury trial is deemed necessary. It is well settled that injunctive relief is not available ***against personal defamation***. In denying relief, the maxim "equity will not enjoin a libel" is frequently cited.

III. EQUITABLE RELIEF IN CONTRACTUAL RELATIONS

A. SPECIFIC PERFORMANCE

1. **In General:** An order granting specific performance is simply a mandatory injunction in a contractual setting. Thus, all of the factors to be considered in discussing injunctions are fully applicable to an action seeking specific performance. In sum, the following conditions must be satisfied before specific performance will be granted:

   a. **The remedy at law is inadequate**;

   b. **The contract is definite and certain**;

   c. **Any conditions precedent are met or excused**;

   d. **Enforcement operates fairly** and

   e. **Enforcement is feasible**.

2. **Mutuality of Remedy No Longer Required:** In earlier decisions, equity courts applied the so-called "negative mutuality" rule wherein specific performance would be denied unless it was available to the other party. This rule is still followed in a minority of states.

   Example: Franchisee cannot sue franchiser for specific performance because franchiser does not have same equitable remedy against franchisee. [See *Florida Jai Alai, Inc. v. Southern Catering*, 388 So. 2d 1076 (Fla. 1980)].

Modern view: Today, an overwhelming majority of states follow the ***mutuality of performance doctrine*** by which specific performance is denied to the injured party only in situations where he has not performed his part of the bargain or where his performance cannot be secured by the decree. In other words, a court of equity will not compel a defendant to perform unless he can be assured of getting the performance promised by the plaintiff.

3. **Money Damages Inadequate:** The plaintiff must show that money damages, the traditional contract remedy, are inadequate to place him in the position he would have been in had the party performed under the provisions of the contract.

4. **Types of Contracts Specifically Enforced:**

   a. **Land sale contracts:** As a general rule, land sale contracts may be specifically enforceable because of the unique character of land. Although some courts have held that specific performance is inappropriate when the seller is suing the buyer, the weight of authority permits specific performance to be awarded to either the seller or the buyer (where, of course, the legal damage remedy proves inadequate).

      i. **Equitable conversion doctrine:** Under an executory real estate sales contract in a majority of jurisdictions, the vendee is regarded as the equitable owner of the property and the vendor is viewed as the equitable owner of the balance of the purchase price.

      Example: Homewanter enters into a contract to buy Blackacre, a lovely home, from Citizen. After the contract is signed but before the actual closing takes place, Blackacre burns down. Under the doctrine of equitable conversion, Homewanter must still pay the purchase price.

      (a) **Buyer's death:** Where the buyer dies before the contract is performed, her heir or devisee may specifically enforce it. The buyer's equitable interest in an enforceable land sale contract is regarded as ***realty*** and that interest descends to the buyer's heir (if an intestacy) or devisee (if there is a will). The duty to pay the purchase price is a contractual obligation that the buyer's executrix or administratrix is required to pay out of the personal estate.

      Example: Gloria Wellbuilt enters into a contract to buy Whiteacre, a beautiful piece of property in Aspen. She dies before closing. Her heirs may enforce the sale, and the seller will be required to sell to them.

      (b) **Seller's death:** By the doctrine of equitable conversion, the seller's beneficial interest in an enforceable land sale contract is regarded as a right to the contract price. That right passes as part of the ***personalty*** to seller's next of kin (if an intestacy) or to her legatee (if there is a will). In either event, the proper party to enforce the contract is the executrix or administratrix of the seller's estate.

Example: Seller enters into a contract to sell Swampacre, a disgusting piece of swamp property. Seller dies before closing, and Buyer uses Seller's death as an opportunity to try to renege on the sale. The executor of Seller's estate may enforce the sale.

ii. **Buyer's remedies for seller's breach of executory land sale contract**

(a) **Damages:** In an action by the buyer against the seller for breach of contract to convey title, two rules have been adopted for measuring damages:

(1) **Benefit of the bargain:** The modern rule followed by a majority of jurisdictions is the "benefit-of-the-bargain" rule and permits the buyer to recover the difference between the contract price and the market value of the land on the date set for performance, plus any partial payments that may have been made, thus protecting the buyer's expectancy interest.

(2) **Out-of-pocket loss:** A minority of states apply the English common law rule limiting the buyer to a recovery of any payments made plus reimbursement of expenses incurred in reliance of the contract (e.g., title search, escrow expenses).

(b) **Specific performance:** As an alternative to the remedy for damages, the buyer may seek specific performance. Once again, equity jurisdiction is based upon the inadequacy of the remedy at law given the uniqueness of land. To be sure, "a compensation in damages will not afford adequate relief, because the peculiar locality, soil, advantages of market, and other conveniences of an estate contracted for cannot be replaced by other land of equal value" (i.e., no two tracts of land are the same). [*Losee v. Morey & Cramer,* 561 Barb. 56 (N.Y., 1865)].

(c) **Liquidated damages provision:** It is important to note that a liquidated damages clause will not necessarily preclude specific performance.

iii. **Seller's remedies for buyer's breach of executory land sale contract**

(a) **Damages:** The seller's damages are the difference between the market value of the land and contract price at the time the buyer's performance was due plus consequential damages.

(b) **Specific performance:** The seller may specifically enforce the contract by seeking a decree ordering the buyer to pay the ***full purchase price.***

(1) **Rationale:** The main reason given why the remedy at law is inadequate is because damages would only give the seller the difference between the contract price and fair market value of the land, and she was bargaining for the full purchase price.

(c) **Rescission and restitution:** Alternatively, the seller may rescind the contract for the buyer's material breach, restoring to the buyer any partial payments made.

b. **Covenants not to compete:** Courts frequently enforce covenants not to compete after termination of an employment contract provided the restriction is ***reasonable*** as to time and place and no broader than necessary to protect the employer.

Example: Steve Mobs signs a non-compete agreement with his employer, Banana Computers. He agrees that, if he leaves Banana Computers, he will not work for any other computer company in the world for 15 years. Such an agreement will NOT be enforceable, as it is not reasonable as to time and place.

Example: Bill Cheapskates signs a non-compete agreement with Microhard agreeing that he will not solicit Microhard's customers if he leaves Microhard for a similar company. Such an agreement is probably enforceable, as it is no broader than necessary to protect the employer.

i. **"Reasonableness" test:** A negative covenant will not be enforced if it is unreasonable (e.g., prevents the defendant from being able to support herself or is too broad). The following factors should be taken into account in analyzing the reasonableness of negative covenants:

(a) **Relationship between parties:**

(1) **Employer-employee;**

(2) **Seller-buyer of a business;**

(3) **Co-partners;**

(4) **Competitors** (and) such a covenant not to compete may violate antitrust laws.

c. **Contracts for the sale of rare or irreplaceable chattels**;

Example: Andrew, a devout Barbra Streisand fan, contracts to buy the tiara that Barbra wore at her wedding. The tiara is one-of-a-kind and is, of course, the only one previously owned by Barbra herself. If Seller Elena (who bought the tiara at a charity auction) changes her mind and decides to keep the tiara, Andrew will be entitled to specific performance and the tiara.

d. **Contracts for the sale of closely held corporate stock for which there is no readily ascertainable market price or that represents the voting control of a corporation that is irreplaceable or unavailable elsewhere;**

e. **Contracts to insure or indemnify when there would be difficulty in getting other insurance;**

f. **Contracts for which damages are too speculative.**

5. **Types of Contracts Not Specifically Enforced:**

a. **Personal service contracts:** Courts rarely decree specific performance of personal service contracts or agreements to form partnerships, marriages, and other business ventures.

i. **Public policy:** It is thought to be against public policy to require the enforcement of continuing business or personal relationships against the will of one of the parties. Arguably, it would even be a violation of the Thirteenth Amendment prohibition of involuntary servitude to force an individual to work in a position against his or her will.

ii. **Supervision problem:** Furthermore, the courts are reluctant to engage in the type of supervision that is necessary in personal service contracts, especially since they cannot guarantee that the defendant will use the requisite skill or expertise bargained for.

(a) **Indirect enforcement:** Although an equity court cannot force a person to work against his or her will, the court may ***indirectly*** enforce a contract for services of an ***exceptionally skilled individual*** (e.g., professional athlete or movie star) by enjoining him or her from working elsewhere.

b. **Employment contracts:** Neither the employer nor the employee may specifically enforce an employment contract. The denial of affirmative relief is based upon the fact that a court cannot realistically supervise enforcement of such a decree.

i. **Damages—breach by employee:** The measure of damages for breach by an employee is the ***cost of obtaining*** equivalent performance by someone else, plus compensation for any consequential damages within the contemplation of the parties when the contract was entered into.

ii. **Damages—breach by employer:** Where the employer's breach is simply a failure to pay wages due under the contract, the non-breaching employee may sue for the amount due.

(a) **Future wages:** Where the employer wrongfully discharges the employee, the employee may recover the total amount of earnings promised ***for full performance*** of the contract, less the amount that the employee earned or could reasonably have earned performing similar services with another employer.

c. **Construction contracts:** As a general rule, specific performance of building contracts is denied. The reason is primarily based upon the belief that there is an adequate remedy at law for damages. Also, equity courts historically are reluctant to issue mandatory injunctions because of the difficulty of enforcement and supervision (e.g., ordering a builder to perform construction work in a workmanlike fashion against his will would be an impossible task).

B. RESCISSION OF CONTRACTS

1. **In General:** Under certain circumstances equity will rescind a contract and render it a nullity, and simultaneously order ***restitution*** to restore the parties to the position they were in before the contract was formed.

2. **Requirements:** It is necessary that the grounds for rescission must occur ***at or before the time*** when the contract was entered into. If this requirement is met, then the contract is ***voidable*** at the option of the affected party.

3. **Grounds:** There are many grounds for rescission:

    a. **Misrepresentation**;

    b. **Mistake**;

    c. **Illegality**;

    d. **Failure of consideration**;

    e. **Lack of capacity**;

    f. **Impossibility of performance**;

    g. **Duress**; and

    h. **Undue influence**.

    Note: Since exam questions dealing with rescission usually/primarily cover misrepresentation and mistake, these grounds are discussed below. The other grounds are covered in the Contracts and Wills Outlines.

4. **Misrepresentation**

    a. **Innocent misrepresentation:** An innocent misrepresentation is ***not*** an actionable tort. As such, there is no recovery at law for money damages. When an innocent misrepresentation is involved, the plaintiff needs to show that the misrepresentation was ***material*** and that she ***reasonably relied*** upon the misrepresentation when entering the contract. Rescission of the contract is proper under such circumstances.

Example: Plaintiff, who loves old Mustangs, contracts to buy a Mustang that Defendant (the seller) tells her is a 1958 model. When the parties enter into the contract, defendant really believes that the Mustang is a 1958 model. Plaintiff has the car inspected by an expert, who determines that the car is a 1957 model, not a 1958. In all other respects, the car is as represented. Plaintiff's request for rescission will probably not be granted, as the misrepresentation was not material (i.e., it is still a vintage car, and the year likely is not different enough to make a significant difference in value).

Example: Plaintiff contracts to purchase an engagement ring for his girlfriend. He picks out a lovely diamond from Jeweler, who tells him (believing it to be true) that the diamond weighs two carats and is internally flawless. After the contract is signed but before Plaintiff picks up the ring, Jeweler discovers that the diamond is actually a cubic zirconia. Rescission would be appropriate under these circumstances, as the misrepresentation that the stone was a diamond was material and Plaintiff relied upon it.

b. **Fraudulent misrepresentation:** Fraudulent misrepresentation occurs when the defendant knowingly (i.e., scienter) makes a false representation that is relied upon to the plaintiff's detriment. The elements of fraudulent misrepresentation are discussed in the Torts Outline. This type of misrepresentation constitutes an actionable tort for which money damages are usually an appropriate remedy. However, rescission is available as an alternative remedy (e.g., the plaintiff has the option of voiding the contract).

Example: Plaintiff contracts to purchase an engagement ring for his girlfriend. He picks out a lovely diamond from Jeweler, who tells him (knowing his statement to be false) that the diamond weighs two carats and is internally flawless. The "diamond" is actually a cubic zirconia. Rescission would be appropriate under these circumstances, as the misrepresentation was fraudulent (knowingly false), and Plaintiff justifiably relied upon it. Note that unlike in an innocent misrepresentation situation Plaintiff would, in the alternative, have an action for damages if he actually went through with the purchase and then discovered the true nature of the stone.

5. **Mistake in Formation of Contract**

a. **Mutual mistake:** In order for rescission to be granted, the mistake must go to the very ***essence*** of the contract. If such a mistake is shown, the contract is voidable and, thus, rescission is the proper remedy.

Example: Grower and Wholesaler enter into a contract for Grower to sell 100 bushels of Yukon Yellow potatoes to Wholesaler. At the time that they enter into the contract, both parties believe that Yukon Yellow potatoes are an existing variety of potato. However, after they have signed the contract, Grower discovers (and communicates to Wholesaler) that Yukon Yellow potatoes are extinct and can no longer be obtained from any source. In this situation, as both parties were mistaken as to an essential element of the contract (the variety of potato) the appropriate remedy is rescission.

b. **Unilateral mistake:** Historically, courts are very reluctant to grant rescission for one party's unilateral mistake. The ***modern trend***, however, is to grant rescission for a unilateral mistake if the mistake is ***material*** and the mistaken party will suffer ***extreme hardship*** by enforcement of the contract or the non-mistaken party had reason to know of the other party's mistake.

Example: Plaintiff is bidding on a contract and makes a miscalculation when composing his bid so that it would be an unreasonable hardship to force him to perform under the bid price.

Example: Plaintiff bids on a toy through an Internet auction. The toy is listed as "Potato Head doll — No reserve!" From the picture of the toy, Plaintiff mistakenly forms the belief that the toy is a Mr. Potato Head doll. However, the toy is actually a Mrs. Potato Head doll. Seller has no reason to know of Plaintiff's misperception, and Plaintiff is the winning bidder, successfully buying the toy for $22.95. Rescission is ***not*** appropriate under these circumstances, as only one party was mistaken and performance of the contract will not cause the Plaintiff extreme hardship.

6. **Restitution**

a. **Tender of consideration:** In order to invoke the rescission remedy, a party must tender back what he has received under the provisions of the contract and, thus, restore the parties to the status quo ante.

7. **Rescission Denied:** As noted in the section on equitable defenses, rescission may be denied due to the following:

a. **Laches**,

b. **Unclean hands**,

c. **Election of remedies**.

C. REFORMATION

1. **In General:** Reformation or "contract revision" is an equitable remedy by which a court modifies or alters a written instrument (e.g., contract or deed) to make it conform to the actual intent of the parties.

a. **Requirements:**

i. **Necessity of valid original contract:** It is necessary that the original contract be free of any defects that would render it voidable.

Exam tip: If the contract is voidable, equity has nothing to reform, and therefore the contract is ***not*** subject to reformation.

ii. **The agreement must be embodied in a writing:** It is impossible to reform an oral agreement.

iii. **The writing fails to express accurately the agreement of the parties.**

2. **Rescission Distinguished:** Reformation is based upon the theory that there was a valid agreement between the parties but that the writing fails to conform to their understanding. In this case, the parties seek to have the equity court reform the writing to reflect the true agreement of the parties. On the other hand, in rescission there is ***no*** valid original contract on account of mistake, misrepresentation, or other avoidance grounds. As such, the original contract is voidable so as to restore the parties to the status quo before the agreement was made.

3. **Grounds for Reformation**

   a. **Fraud:** If one party to a contract induces the other party to execute the agreement by fraudulently misrepresenting the document's contents, reformation will be granted.

   b. **Mutual mistake:** Reformation will be granted where both parties are mutually mistaken or unaware that the written instrument constitutes a deviation from their original oral agreement.

   Example: Parties orally agree that the sale price for certain goods will be $599.95. However, both parties sign a written contract unaware that the price was incorrectly listed as $5,995. The court will reform the contract to reflect the agreed-upon price.

   Example: Parties orally agree that the date of performance will be June 30, 2000. However, both parties sign a written contract unaware that the date of performance is incorrectly listed as June 30, 1900 (a Y2K error). The court will reform the contract to list the correct date.

   c. **Unilateral mistake:** If either party knows or has reason to know that the written instrument does not embody the true agreement (and the other party is unaware of the error), reformation will be granted.

   d. **Mistake in inducement not applicable:** It is important to distinguish between mistake in the inducement to a contract and mistake in the execution.

      i. **Mistake in inducement distinguishable:** Reformation is only available to correct mistakes or errors in the execution of a contract (or those which occur in putting the agreement in writing). It is not the proper remedy where either party claims to have made a mistake in entering into the contract. If the mistake is in the inducement, such cases must be analyzed under rescission, supra.

4. **Defenses**

   a. **Laches** (See Section IV.A. supra)

   b. **Sale to bona fide purchaser:** The right to reformation will be cut off where the subject matter of the instrument to be reformed is sold to a purchaser for value without notice of the right to reformation.

   c. **Parol evidence rule:** Clearly, the parol evidence rule ***cannot*** be a valid defense to reformation. This is so because if it were applicable the court could not discover what the original agreement of the parties was.

   d. **Statute of Frauds:** In certain situations, the Statute of Frauds may be a valid defense in reformation proceedings. If the written agreement, for example, fails to comply with any of the technical requirements of the Statute of Frauds (e.g., land sale contract not signed by the vendor), it typically cannot be reformed.

      i. **Part performance doctrine:** However, the harshness of this rule is somewhat rectified by the doctrine of part performance, which will allow reformation to be had if the plaintiff has substantially performed her part of the contract (i.e., payment of the purchase price and taken possession of the property).

         Example: Example: Vendor and Vendee orally contract for the purchase of Whiteacre for $100,000. The parties sign a contract that inadvertently omits the price. Ordinarily, the Statute of Frauds would prevent reformation of the writing to include this missing essential term. However, if Vendee has paid the price and taken possession of Whiteacre, the contract may be reformed.

   e. **Negligence:** According to the majority view, reformation will not be denied simply because the party seeking it is chargeable with negligence (e.g., failure to read the contract).

      Example: As in the immediately preceding example, Vendor orally contracts with Vendee to purchase a car for $100,000. When the agreement is reduced to writing, a typographical error is made so that the contract reads "10,000." Vendor does not carefully read the contract, which was typed by his secretary. This failure to read the contract will not preclude Vendor's claim for reformation.

IV. SPECIAL EQUITABLE DEFENSES

A. CLEAN HANDS AND LACHES

1. **Clean Hands:** Whenever a plaintiff seeks equitable relief, she must be free of any wrongdoing as it relates to the defendant and the subject matter of the litigation. Thus, the maxim "one who comes into equity must come with clean hands."

   a. **Wrongdoing must relate to same transaction:** The plaintiff's prior wrongful conduct must relate to the particular transaction for which relief is sought and must prejudice or injure the defendant. Prior wrongdoing unrelated to the issue or the parties does ***not*** bar the plaintiff's suit.

   Example: Plaintiff sues to enjoin a nuisance. The defendant cannot forestall an injunction by introducing evidence that plaintiff acquired title to the property after killing his mother.

   Compare: Relief may be denied in an action to enjoin unfair competition when the good will that plaintiff is seeking to protect was built up by false advertising.

   b. **Exception—"public fraud":** An exception to the foregoing rule is found where the plaintiff's unclean hands (e.g., fraud) is not directed against the defendant but affects the general public.

   Example: A real estate broker, who is not licensed to practice, brings suit for specific performance against defendant seeking to enforce a brokerage agreement. Here, relief will be denied because broker's failure to be properly licensed constitutes a public fraud.

2. **Laches:** Laches is an equity doctrine to the effect that an ***unreasonable*** delay in initiating or pursuing a claim will bar plaintiff's cause of action if the delay results in prejudice to the defendant.

   a. **In relation to the statute of limitations:** In most states, the statute of limitations is applicable to suits in equity as well as at law. In cases where the statute has not run, laches may still bar plaintiff's suit before the expiration of the period of limitations.

   b. **No bar to action at law:** Laches is strictly an equitable doctrine and cannot be used to defeat a legal claim for money damages.

   c. **Time when laches starts to run:** Generally speaking, laches begins to run from the time when the plaintiff has ***knowledge*** that a right has been infringed.

   d. **Application:** Laches is predicated upon the maxim "equity aids the vigilant." Although it arises by the effect of delay, there are no precise rules governing its application. Rather, each case must be determined by its own facts and circumstances.

Exam tip: The defense of laches is applicable to all equitable actions and should be taken into account when discussing specific performance, injunctions, rescission, and reformation as well as constructive trusts.

B. UNDUE HARDSHIP

1. **In General:** There are situations where a plaintiff has made out a case for equitable relief but undue harm would result to the defendant by granting the requested remedy. In such cases, the equity court may deny relief and leave the plaintiff to his remedy at law, if available.

2. **Specific Performance Cases:** As discussed earlier, the equitable conversion doctrine attaches at the moment the vendor and vendee enter into their real estate sales contract. The traditional view is that the risk of loss from destruction of the premises is placed on the buyer after the contract is executed. Thus, a seller may specifically enforce the contract despite the fact that the premises are destroyed by fire or flood.

   a. **Exception:** However, under the doctrine of frustration of purpose, if the buyer's intended use of the property is known to the seller and rendered unattainable by some supervening act, then the equity court may deny specific performance to avoid undue hardship to the buyer.

3. **Injunction Cases:** In injunction cases, undue hardship is sometimes considered by "balancing the equities." In this process, the equity court considers the hardship to each party that would result if the relief were granted or denied.

   a. **Note:** In industrial nuisance cases, for example, the court will not enjoin the operation of a factory if the economic consequences to defendant greatly outweigh any gain the plaintiff may get from the decree. Frequently in these cases, the injury to the public (e.g., loss of jobs and economic hardship on the community) is a primary factor in the balancing process. In such a case, the plaintiff is limited to its remedy at law, if any.

   b. **Encroachment cases:** As noted previously, the doctrine of undue hardship is commonly invoked in encroachment cases to prevent issuance of injunctive relief.

   Example: Defendant's ten-story apartment building has a three-foot encroachment over plaintiff's property line. The court will deny plaintiff's suit seeking an injunction requiring defendant to totally demolish her building.

V. SPECIAL FORMS OF EQUITABLE RELIEF

A. SUIT TO QUIET TITLE

1. **In General:** In a suit to quiet title (or a bill to remove cloud on title), a plaintiff possessing land seeks to vindicate his or her interest by having the court clear title to the property.

    a. **Note:** Only legal titles may be quieted, i.e., a holder of an equitable claim may not file against the holder of the legal title. Also, courts frequently hold that a suit to quiet title is restricted to a party in possession since ejectment is an adequate legal remedy for one out of possession.

B. CONSTRUCTIVE TRUST

1. **Nature of Remedy:** Constructive trusts do not arise because of the express intent of a settlor, but are "fraud-rectifying" trusts created by operation of law ***to prevent unjust enrichment***. The constructive trust is similar to a quasi-contractual form of relief in that both are imposed by law ***without regard to the intention of the parties*** to compel the restoration of unjust gains.

    a. **Operation of rule:** Basically, the imposition of a constructive trust results in a transfer of legal ownership of the property (*res*) from the defendant (constructive trustee) to the plaintiff. Restoration of unjust enrichment is the sole obligation of the defendant as constructive trustee, and this obligation is enforced by mandatory injunction.

    b. **Requirements:**

        i. The defendant has legal title to specific property (*res*) which rightfully belongs to the claimant;

        ii. The retention of the property by defendant would result in ***unjust enrichment***;

        iii. The remedy at law is inadequate (usually insolvency of the defendant satisfies this requirement).

        Exam tip: While the concept of constructive trust is rather simple, it is often overlooked by students. As a consequence, it is a favorite exam topic that should be discussed whenever appropriate. Always look to see whether the defendant is rightfully entitled to the property in question. In the event he is not (i.e., he is unjustly enriched) consider the remedy of constructive trust making the possessor a trustee for the equitable owner.

    c. **Effect of sale to bona fide purchaser:** A transfer to a bona fide purchaser, who pays value without notice of the facts giving rise to the constructive trust, cuts off plaintiff's right to a constructive trust to the item so transferred. It is important to note, however, that the transfer does ***not*** cut off plaintiff's rights against the ***proceeds*** obtained by the defendant from the transfer.

C. EQUITABLE LIENS

1. **Definition:** A lien is a charge against property that makes the property stand as security for debts or obligations owed. Equitable liens may be created either by agreement or by judicial proceedings. In effect, an equitable lien is a ***restitutionary remedy*** imposed by the equity court to avoid unjust enrichment.

    a. **Compare to constructive trust:** The holder of an equitable lien cannot recover specific property as can the beneficiary of a constructive trust. Thus, the constructive trust gives complete title to the claimant whereas the equitable lien only creates a security interest in the property which can be used to satisfy the debt.

        i. **Application:** Quite often the aggrieved party will have a ***choice*** of imposing an equitable lien or constructive trust over defendant's property.

        Example: Defendant embezzles money from plaintiff, which he uses to buy Blackacre. Plaintiff has the election of imposing a constructive trust over the said property (in which case she recovers the land) or creating an equitable lien as security for the amount misappropriated.

        Contrast: Defendant, who is already in ownership of Blackacre, embezzles money from plaintiff. The misappropriated funds are used by defendant to improve his property. In this situation, plaintiff's only remedy is to impose an equitable lien on Blackacre. Since the money was not used to acquire the property, the plaintiff cannot claim title by way of a constructive trust.

    b. **Effect of sale to bona fide purchaser:** An equitable lien is ***cut off*** by transfer of the property to a bona fide purchaser.

D. SUBROGATION

1. **Definition:** Subrogation is an equitable doctrine applied where one party discharges an obligation for which another is primarily liable and that the latter ought to pay. It is allowed in situations where an unjust or inequitable benefit is conferred on the defendant.

    a. **In general:** Subrogation is accomplished by reviving in equity, for the benefit of the aggrieved party, an obligation similar to the one discharged. The plaintiff is said to be subrogated to the position of the creditor. Therefore, the interests acquired by the plaintiff (referred to as the subrogee) depend upon the nature of the original claim.

Example: A, by mistake, pays a secured debt owed by B to C. A is entitled to be subrogated to the position C held prior to payment and thus both debt and security are revived for the benefit of A.

VI. RESTITUTIONARY REMEDIES

A. REPLEVIN

1. **Basis:** Replevin is an "***action at law*** for the recovery of specific chattels that have been wrongfully taken or detained."

   a. **Possessory action:** The gist of replevin is that it is a possessory action permitting the plaintiff to recover immediate possession of the property (at the beginning of the action).

      i. **Plaintiff must post bond:** Where the plaintiff wants to recover the chattel at the beginning of the action, he must post a bond as security. This bond protects the defendant in case judgment is rendered in his favor. Note that defendant may post bond if he wishes to retain the chattel until the action has concluded.

      ii. **Pre-seizure hearing required:** No seizure of the chattel is allowed until a hearing has taken place to determine plaintiff's entitlement to the chattel. [*Fuentes v. Shevin*, 407 U.S. 67 (1972)].

   b. **Types of property:** Replevin may be brought to recover specific chattels or other tangible personal property. It will not lie for recovery of real property or intangible personal property.

   c. **Damages also available:** Note that any damages suffered from the deprivation may also be recovered.

      i. **Measure of damages:** The measure of damages is either the market value of the chattel at the time of the deprivation minus the market value at the time the action is commenced (if the chattel is held for sale) ***or*** the value of lost use (rental value or lost profits).

   d. **If the chattel is not returned:** Where judgment is for plaintiff but the chattel is not returned, the plaintiff recovers the present value of the chattel as established at trial.

   e. **Adverse possession precludes recovery:** Note that, where the defendant has acquired title through adverse possession, replevin is not available.

      i. Mere possession not enough. The possession — even long-term possession — must be open and notorious, hostile, adverse, and visible.

f. **Equitable replevin:** If the defendant secreted the chattel or removed it from the jurisdiction, and it could not be seized, then this form of injunction may issue.

B. EJECTMENT

1. **In General:** Ejectment is an "***action at law*** to recover possession of real property."
2. **Essential Elements:**
   a. **Proof of legal title**

   b. **Proof of right to possession** and

   c. **Wrongful withholding by the defendant.**
3. **Damages:** A successful plaintiff is entitled to judgment for recovery of the property and for mesne damages. Mesne damages compensate for the loss of use of the land and are measured by the rental value of the property or the benefit gained by the wrongful possessor, whichever is greater.
4. **Effects of Improvements to Property by Defendant:** At common law, where the defendant trespasses on or takes possession of plaintiff's property and makes improvements thereon, the plaintiff is entitled to recover the property and need not compensate the defendant for these improvements. This is true even though the defendant acted in good faith, ***mistakenly*** believing that he had rightful possession of the property. Note that, modernly, many jurisdictions have provided defendant with some recourse, from (1) the right to claim setoff where plaintiff seeks mesne damages to (2) equitable relief for unjust enrichment to (3) the right for defendant to remove who acted in good faith or seek compensation for the improvement to (4) the imposition of an equitable lien on the property to (5) the right for defendant to buy the property from plaintiff if they so agree.

C. QUASI-CONTRACT

1. **Nature of Action:** Quasi-contracts, or contracts implied-in-law, are restitutionary actions designed ***to prevent unjust enrichment***. Quasi-contracts cover situations where the parties have ***not*** entered into a contract but the court imposes an obligation on the part of the defendant to repay the Plaintiff "for goods sold and delivered" *(quantum valebat)*; or "for work and labor performed" *(quantum meruit)*; or "for money had and received."

   Example: Clark contracts to have Landscaper plant trees and shrubs in her backyard. Clark lives at 100 Ocean Avenue. On the date of performance, Landscaper by mistake goes to Mitchell's home at 1000 Ocean Avenue and performs the landscaping work. After realizing his error, Landscaper attempts to reenter Mitchell's backyard to remove the improvements. Mitchell refuses to permit Landscaper to come back onto the property and threatens to injure him if he does so. Immediately thereafter, Landscaper brings a restitutionary action against Mitchell seeking to recover the reasonable value of the trees and shrubs that were planted. Although no actual contract exists between the parties, the court will "imply" a contract (i.e., quasi-contract) and order Mitchell to pay Landscaper in order to prevent unjust enrichment.

D. IMPLIED-IN-FACT CONTRACT

1. **Basis:** Implied-in-fact contracts are actual contracts which are created by the ***conduct*** of the parties, e.g., raising one's hand at an auction to bid for goods.

   Example: Guest regularly eats in a local diner. Each week, he orders the Thursday special, meatloaf with mashed potatoes and green beans. This special does not come with dessert. If Waitress brings Guest a piece of pecan pie (without Guest's requesting it) and Guest eats it, Guest must pay for it under the doctrine of implied-in-fact contract.

VII. MONEY DAMAGES

A. PURPOSE OF DAMAGES

1. **Tort Damages.** The purpose of tort damages is to place the injured party in a position similar to that he would have been in had the wrong not occurred, i.e., to compensate him for injury suffered.

2. **Contract Damages.** The objective behind contract damages is to place the non-breaching party in the position he would have been in had the contract been fully performed.

B. COMPENSATORY DAMAGES

1. **Adequate Remedy at Law:** This remedy provides an award of damages in the form of a money judgment to the aggrieved party to compensate for any loss or injury. It is recognized as a substitutionary form of relief in that it gives the plaintiff money by way of compensation.

   a. **Tort theory:** In tort cases, the objective of damages is to make the plaintiff whole by awarding money to make up for his loss or injury. There are certain torts (such as intentional infliction of mental distress, false imprisonment, and defamation) in which no pecuniary harm is actually done. Nonetheless, the courts have granted compensatory damages to vindicate a legal right that has been wrongfully infringed.

      i. **General damages:** General damages are those that arise naturally from the commission of a tort. They do not need to be pleaded specially in a complaint. General damages are presumed to flow from the tort, thus no separate showing of foreseeability is required.

ii. **Special damages:** Special damages must be pleaded specially. The plaintiff must show that his injury was caused by the defendant and that all injuries stemming from the wrong will be attributed to the defendant. Foreseeability is required to recover special damages. Finally, the plaintiff must be able to prove his damages; no speculation is allowed.

iii. **Pain and suffering:** Compensatory damages are also allowed for pain and suffering, which is another form of non-pecuniary harm recognized by the law.

b. **Contracts theory:** In contracts cases, the objective of damages is not only to compensate for loss but also to protect the plaintiff's expectation interest by awarding a sum of money equivalent to what he would have received had the contract been performed.

i. **General damages:** In contract disputes, general damages are those that arise naturally from a breach. As in tort actions, they do not need to be pleaded specially.

ii. **Special damages:** As in tort cases, foreseeability, certainty, and causation are required. It is generally easier to quantify harm (e.g., economic injury) in contracts cases. Note that this may not always be true (e.g., where the plaintiff must attempt to prove lost profits from a newly established business).

c. **Real property theory:** The goal of damages involving injury to real property is that of compensation. There are two alternative rules with respect to the measurement of damages:

i. **Cost of repair:** The cost of repair rule entitles the injured party to recover the cost of restoring the realty to its condition immediately prior to the injury.

ii. **Diminution in value:** This measure of damages entitles the injured party to recover the difference between the value of the real property immediately before and immediately after the injury.

2. **Amount recoverable.** The amount of compensatory damages recoverable may be limited by several rules of law.

a. **Reasonable certainty.** All contract damages must be proven with reasonable certainty and cannot be too speculative.

b. **Avoidable consequences rule.** The plaintiff is required to mitigate special damages. Where he does not, he may not recover the damages he could have avoided incurring through reasonable acts. This rule applies in tort and in contract.

c. **Collateral source rule.** If a plaintiff gets benefits from a collateral source (i.e., not the defendant) in a tort or contract action, the defendant may not claim these benefits to reduce his own liability. In other words, in some cases, the plaintiff may recover twice, once from the collateral source, once from the defendant. However, he may not recover twice if the first set of benefits derived from the defendant or his agent. Frequently the collateral source will be subrogated to the plaintiff's recovery thus avoiding double recovery.

Example: Plaintiff brings an action against defendant for $20,000 in medical expenses. Plaintiff was insured at the time of the accident that caused his injuries, and his insurance company paid all medical expenses. Plaintiff may still sue defendant for the medical expenses and collect the full amount if he prevails on the liability issue. Plaintiff's insurance company may be subrogated to the amount the plaintiff receives from the defendant for the medical expenses, requiring plaintiff to turn over these monies to his insurance company.

Example: Plaintiff brings an action against defendant for $20,000 in medical expenses. At the time of the accident that caused his injuries, plaintiff did not have medical insurance. However, defendant arranged for his insurance company to pay plaintiff's medical expenses. Plaintiff may not bring a claim against defendant for the $20,000, as defendant's insurance company paid the expenses as defendant's agent.

i. **Types of benefits to which the collateral source rule applies:**

(a) **Insurance policies**, whether maintained by the plaintiff or by a third party for plaintiff's benefit;

(b) **Employment benefits**;

(c) **Gratuities** (this applies to cash gratuities and to the rendering of services, e.g., plaintiff being treated at a veteran's hospital);

(d) **Social legislation benefits**. Note the collateral source rule may be changed by statute or the provider may be subrogated to plaintiff's recovery for the benefits paid.

C. NOMINAL DAMAGES

1. **Basis:** Nominal damages are awarded in situations where the plaintiff's rights have been violated, but ***no loss is sustained*** or the extent of injury cannot be measured.

D. PUNITIVE DAMAGES

1. **In General:** A sum of money may be awarded in tort in addition to compensatory damages to punish the defendant for willful, wanton, or malicious conduct and to act as a deterrent against such future conduct.

2. **Discretionary:** A plaintiff is never entitled to an award of punitive damages, but a jury may award them at its discretion. Jury rewards may be reversed or overturned if excessive.

3. **Not Available in Contract Actions:** Punitive damages are not available in contract actionsunless such damages are provided by statute or the defendant's actions constitute a separate actionable tort justifying an award of punitive damages, such as fraud.

E. INTEREST

1. **Types of Interest:** There are two types of interest, Pre-judgment and Post-judgment.

   a. **Pre-judgment interest:** Pre-judgment interest is calculated from the time the injury occurred to the date of judgment.

   b. **Post-judgment interest:** Post-judgment interest is calculated from the time the judgment is entered. Post-judgment interest is awarded more often than pre-judgment interest.

2. **Concept Governing Interest Awards:** In awarding interest, the court seeks to compensate the plaintiff for interest he would have earned had he invested the money during the time defendant had dispossessed him of it. The interest rate in effect at the time is applied.

3. **Interest Is Not Awarded in Speculative Situations:** For example, interest is not awarded for pain and suffering, mental distress, or other difficult-to-quantify claims.

F. ATTORNEY'S FEES

1. **Concept Governing Attorney's Fees:** Generally, attorney's fees are awarded when a contract provides for them or when defendant has brought an action in bad faith. They may also be available under various statutes (e.g., civil rights statutes) and in shareholder derivative suits (where the shareholder has brought a suit on behalf of the shareholders).

G. LIQUIDATED DAMAGES

1. **Definition:** Liquidated damages are those provided for by contract between the parties. They are appropriate when the parties anticipate that a breach of the underlying contract may occur but that damages in the event of such a breach would be difficult to calculate. The amount agreed upon must be a reasonable prediction of what the damages would be.

2. **Validity:** Liquidated damages provisions are generally held to be valid if the actual damages are genuinely difficult to calculate and if they are reasonable.

Liquidated damages which are a penalty in disguise (i.e., those disproportionate to the actual damages and that are designed to punish the breaching party) will be rejected by the courts.

3. **Only Enforced When Damage Occurs:** Liquidated damages provisions are not enforced when there are no damages, even if the contemplated breach occurs. In other words, it is not enough for one party to breach; in order for the liquidated damages provision to be enforceable, the non-breaching party must actually be damaged.

4. **Not a Bar to Specific Performance:** Even where the parties have a contract containing a liquidated damages clause, this clause will not prevent the non-breaching party from requesting—or the court from granting—specific performance where such a remedy is otherwise appropriate (i.e., money damages will not suffice to right the wrong).

    a. **Exception:** If the parties have stipulated in the contract that the liquidated damages will be the ***only*** available remedy, a court may decline to order specific performance even if it is otherwise appropriate.

TRUE-FALSE QUESTION TOPIC LIST

1. When equitable remedies are available
2. Speculative nature of money damages
3. Judicial discretion
4. Specific performance of employment contracts
5. Mandatory injunctions
6. Mandatory vs. prohibitory injunctions
7. *Ex parte* motions
8. Length of temporary restraining orders
9. Enforceability of injunctions
10. Injunctions in privacy cases
11. Converted property
12. Incorporeal interests in land — appropriateness of injunctions
13. Encroachment
14. Remedy for simple trespass
15. Enjoinment of crimes
16. Remedy for permissive waste
17. Remedy for ameliorating waste
18. Enforceability of agreements not to disclose
19. Equitable relief in marital disputes
20. Mutuality of remedy
21. Specific performance for land sale contracts
22. Enforceability of covenants not to compete
23. Enforceability of building contracts
24. Availability of rescission remedy
25. Rescission as an appropriate remedy for mutual mistake
26. Reformation of oral contracts

27. Mistake and reformation
28. Defenses — unclean hands
29. Defenses — laches
30. Defenses — undue hardship
31. Constructive trusts
32. Equitable liens
33. Replevin
34. Ejectment
35. Quasi-contract
36. Claims for special damages
37. Availability of punitive damages
38. Proof of damages
39. Avoidable consequences rule
40. Collateral source rule

TRUE-FALSE QUESTIONS

For each of the following questions, circle True ("T") or False ("F")

1. T F Equitable remedies are only available where there is no adequate remedy at law.

2. T F If plantiff suffers harm but the calculation of damages is too speculative, then equitable relief is likely to be available.

3. T F Where damages are not an adequate remedy, a judge must grant an equitable remedy when it is requested.

4. T F Employment contracts are specifically enforceable.

5. T F A mandatory injunction is one that requires a defendant to perform an affirmative act.

6. T F Courts prefer to issue mandatory injunctions (versus prohibitory injunctions).

7. T F A preliminary injunction may be issued *ex parte*.

8. T F A temporary restraining order is typically issued for about 5 days.

9. T F An injunction generally must be enforceable by the court or the court will decline to grant it.

10. T F Injunctive relief is not available in privacy cases.

11. T F A court does not have the power to order a defendant to return converted property.

12. T F Incorporeal interests in land are considered to be unique and, therefore, an equitable remedy is appropriate when there has been unreasonable interference with such an interest.

13. T F If a defendant inadvertently builds on plaintiff's property, the court will probably require the defendant to tear the building down.

14. T F Nominal damages are appropriate for simple acts of trespass.

15. T F Courts will generally enjoin the ongoing commission of crimes.

16. T F Where inaction results in damage to property, money damages are the appropriate remedy.

17. T F When a tenant alters property in a beneficial way, an injunction is the appropriate remedy.

18. T F Where an employee signs an agreement not to divulge trade secrets to those outside of the company, such an agreement is specifically enforceable.

19. T F Equitable relief is generally available to restrain a spouse's immoral conduct.

20. T F Most jurisdictions require that specific performance is only available to the plaintiff where it is also available to the defendant.

21. T F Land sale contracts are usually specifically enforceable.

22. T F Even broadly drafted covenants not to compete are specifically enforceable.

23. T F Building contracts are generally specifically enforceable.

24. T F As long as the grounds for the remedy occur before an action is begun, rescission is an available remedy.

25. T F In a situation involving mutual mistake as to an essential element of a contract, rescission is an appropriate remedy.

26. T F Oral agreements are capable of reformation.

27. T F Reformation is not the appropriate remedy when either party claims to have made a mistake in entering into a contract.

28. T F To seek equitable relief, the plaintiff must be free of any wrongdoing with respect to the transaction.

29. T F The defendant need not bring an action for equitable relief within any particular time frame.

30. T F Even if a plaintiff has made out a good case for equitable relief, the court may still deny his claim if it would cause the defendant undue hardship.

31. T F The imposition of a constructive trust results in the transfer of legal ownership of the property from the defendant to the plaintiff.

32. T F As with a constructive trust, the holder of an equitable lien may recover specific property.

33. T F In a replevin proceeding, the plaintiff may recover the chattel in question at the beginning of the action.

34. T F At common law, where the defendant made improvements to property not rightfully his, the plaintiff could eject the defendant from the property and keep the improvements without compensation to the defendant.

35. T F Restitution is an appropriate remedy where there has been a quasi-contract between the parties.

36. T F Foreseeability is required where special damages are claimed.

37. T F Punitive damages are available against the breaching party in a contract action.

38. T F For the purpose of establishing damages, it is harder to prove harm in contracts cases than in torts cases.

39. T F A plaintiff may not recover damages he could have avoided through reasonable acts.

40. T F A plaintiff may recover damages twice, once from the defendant and once from the defendant's insurance company.

ANSWERS TO TRUE-FALSE QUESTIONS

1. **True.**

   In order to grant equitable relief, the court must find the absence of an adequate legal remedy. Note that this does not mean that legal remedies are not also recoverable, rather, simply that, on their own, they will not compensate plaintiff for the harm he has suffered.

2. **True.**

   Where damages are so speculative that any money award is likely to be inadequate, equitable relief is appropriate.

3. **False.**

   Equitable relief is largely a matter of judicial discretion.

4. **False.**

   Employment contracts are not specifically enforceable because of the difficulty of supervising enforcement of the decree and the undesirability of imposing an employment relationship on persons who are in serious disagreement.

5. **True.**

6. **False.**

   Courts prefer to issue prohibitory injunctions, because these are easier to monitor and because the court may easily sanction a defendant who has continued to do a prohibited act.

7. **False.**

   A temporary restraining order may be issued *ex parte*, but a preliminary injunction is only issued after notice to the defendant and an adversary hearing.

8. **False.**

   A typical temporary restraining order lasts about ten days or until the hearing on the preliminary injunction, whichever comes first.

9. **True.**

   Note that this is usually more of a problem with mandatory injunctions than with prohibitory injunctions.

10. **False.**

    While equitable relief used to be denied in privacy cases, now the court will look to the adequacy of legal remedies. If the invasion is a continuing one, the court may issue an injunction, but if the harm was a one-time occurrence, then money damages will probably compensate the plaintiff for the harm he has suffered.

11. False.

While replevin or money damages will compensate for ordinary chattels, a mandatory injunction is the appropriate remedy for the conversion of a unique chattel.

12. True.

This rule applies to easements, profits, and other non-possessory interests in land.

13. False.

Under these circumstances, the defendant's cost of removal of the encroachment may far exceed the value of the land restored to the plaintiff. Thus, courts balance the hardships in determining whether equitable relief should be granted.

14. True.

Usually such a trespass will cause little or no damage to the property thus limiting the remedy to nominal damages.

15. False.

Police action and criminal prosecution are considered the appropriate actions in the case of ongoing crime.

16. True.

Usually the damages will be based on the cost of repairs.

17. False.

Since it is not possible to show irreparable injury (or, indeed, any injury), the court will not restrain beneficial action on the part of a tenant.

18. True.

This type of employment contract is common and is considered valid by most courts.

19. False.

The vast majority of courts agree in their belief that the problem of extramarital conduct cannot be resolved by the use of injunctions.

20. False.

This old "mutuality of remedy" rule is no longer applied in most jurisdictions. Modernly, specific performance (where appropriate) is denied to the injured party only in situations where he has not performed his part of the bargain or where his performance cannot be secured by the decree.

21. True.

This rule applies because each parcel of land is considered to be unique. Although some courts have held that specific performance is inappropriate when the seller is suing the buyer, the weight of authority permits specific performance to be awarded to either the seller or the buyer.

22. False.

To be enforceable, a covenant not to compete must be reasonable as to time and place and no broader than necessary to protect the employer.

23. False.

Generally, courts hold that there is an adequate remedy at law for damages. Also, equity courts are reluctant to issue mandatory injunctions because of the difficulty of enforcement and supervision.

24. False.

It is necessary that the grounds for rescission must occur at or before the time that the contract was entered into.

25. True.

If such a mistake is shown, the contract is voidable and, thus, rescission is the proper remedy.

26. False.

Reformation is an equitable remedy by which a court modifies or alters a written instrument to make it conform to the actual intent of the parties.

27. True.

If one party feels that the original contract (as agreed to orally) was a mistake, there was no meeting of the minds. The dispute is then as to the validity of the agreement and not as to whether the written agreement correctly reflects the elements of the oral one. Rescission would therefore be the correct remedy, not reformation.

28. True.

Whenever a plaintiff seeks equitable relief, she must be free of any wrongdoing as it relates to the defendant and the subject matter of the litigation.

29. False.

An unreasonable delay in initiating or pursuing a claim will bar plaintiff's cause of action under the doctrine of laches if the delay results in prejudice to the defendant.

30. True.

There are situations where a plaintiff has made out a case for equitable relief but undue harm would result to the defendant by granting the requested remedy. In such cases, the equity court may deny relief and leave the plaintiff to his remedy at law, if available.

31. True.

Restoration of unjust enrichment is the sole obligation of the defendant as constructive trustee, and this obligation is enforced by mandatory injunction.

32. False.

The equitable lien only creates a security interest in the property that can be used to satisfy a debt.

33. True.

Replevin is a possessory action permitting the plaintiff to recover immediate possession of the property. Note that, where the plaintiff wants to recover the chattel at the beginning of the action, he must post bond for it.

34. True.

Modernly, however, many jurisdictions provide a defendant who acted in good faith with some recourse and hope for compensation.

35. True.

Contracts implied-in-law are restitutionary actions designed to prevent unjust enrichment.

36. True.

The plaintiff must show that his injury was caused by the defendant and that all injuries stemming from the wrong will be attributed to the defendant, who was able to foresee the consequences of his actions.

37. False.

In the vast majority of jurisdictions, punitive damages are not available in contract actions.

38. False.

Actually, the opposite is true, as tort cases are often based on "fuzzy" concepts like emotional distress, whereas contracts cases are based on language in an agreement and generally deal with ascertainable economic relationships.

39. True.

This is called the Avoidable Consequences Rule or the duty to mitigate damages.

40. False.

The Collateral Source Rule doesn't apply to payments made by the defendant or the defendant's insurance company. Under the Collateral Source Rule plaintiff can recover twice if one recovery is from his own insurance company (or another collateral source) and one is from the defendant.

MULTIPLE CHOICE QUESTION TOPIC LIST

1. Remedies for implied-in-fact contracts
2. Specific performance for the sale of unique property
3. Mutual mistake–rescission
4. Recovery of reasonable value of services rendered
5. Recovery for non-conforming goods/Statute of Frauds
6. Recovery before total breach
7. Measuring damages
8. Specific performance in employment contracts
9. Remedies for nuisance
10. Remedies in contracts to manufacture special goods
11. Measuring damages
12. Calculation of damages/incidental damages/consequential damages/specific performance
13. Calculation of damages/incidental damages
14. Measuring damages
15. Entitlement to damages
16. Damages/quantum meruit/restitution
17. Restitution/quantum meruit
18. Expectancy/specific performance/calculation of damages–construction -contracts
19. Loss of bargain
20. Liquidated damages
21. Specific performance/nominal damages
22. Injunction/encroachment
23. Rescission/mistake
24. Rescission/mistake
25. Specific performance

REMEDIES

26. Recovery of prepayment/mitigation of damages
27. Incidental damages/punitive damages/consequential damages
28. Calculation of damages/incidental damages
29. Remedies—construction contracts
30. Expectation damages
31. Calculation of damages–construction contracts
32. Restitution/unjust enrichment
33. Incorporeal interests in land/injunctions
34. Ameliorating waste/injunctions
35. Ameliorating waste/damages

Question 1 refers to the following fact pattern.

Deke Deaver hired Sidney Snead, a golf pro, to give lessons to his 14-year-old son, Drake. Deke agreed to pay Sidney $1,000 for ten lessons, which were to be held on Saturday mornings from 10:00 A.M. to 11:00 A.M. When Drake and Deke arrived for the first lesson, they were accompanied by Drake's 6-year-old younger brother, Desmond. As Sidney started his instructional lesson with Drake, Desmond asked if he could participate. Sidney did not object and allowed Desmond to receive instructions along with his brother.

As it turned out, Desmond accompanied Drake and took all ten lessons with his older brother. Each Saturday Deke was present and watched Sidney give the same lessons to both boys. After Desmond and Drake received their last lesson, Sidney requested payment. When Deke presented a check for $1,000, Sidney told Deke that he owed an additional $1,000 for the lessons that Desmond received. After Deke refused to pay for Desmond's lessons, Sidney brought a contract action against Deke for $1,000.

1. Deke will most likely be held liable for

    (A) nothing, because Sidney allowed Desmond to gratuitously participate in the lessons.
    (B) nothing, because no formal contract was entered into between Sidney and Deke.
    (C) $1,000, because an implied-in-fact contract was formed.
    (D) the reasonable value of services rendered, as measured by Desmond's improvement.

Question 2 refers to the following fact pattern.

Crooner was an opera singer who collected rare recordings of opera stars from the 1920s. Collette owned a collection of many old opera recordings that she had inherited from her grandfather. Collette learned of Crooner's interest in rare opera recordings and offered to sell Crooner an opera recording from an obscure tenor, Ralphio, who died after only one recorded performance. Crooner was anxious to obtain the recording because there were no other known copies of a Ralphio recorded performance and it would make Crooner's collection complete. Crooner offered Collette $10,000 for the Ralphio recording subject to certification by Prof. Erickson, a recognized expert in the subject of 20th-century opera singers. Collette wrote to Crooner and accepted the offer. Prior to submitting the recording to Prof. Erickson for certification, Collette received an offer of $20,000 from another collector for the Ralphio recording. Collette told Prof. Erickson that the Ralphio recording was a fake so she could take advantage of the offer from the collector. Prof. Erickson refused to issue the certificate, and Crooner rejected Collette's tender of the recording when she presented it without the certificate.

2. If Crooner discovers the reason why Prof. Erickson would not certify the recording and brings suit against Collette, Crooner may recover

    (A) nothing, because Crooner rejected Collette's tender of the recording.
    (B) money damages only, measured by the difference between the contract and the market price.
    (C) an injunction only, to prevent the sale to the collector.
    (D) specific performance.

Question 3 refers to the following fact pattern.

Player, an experienced antique collector, orally agreed to pay Stringer $250,000 for a rare Stradivarius violin. During their negotiations, both parties referred to the violin as "an original Stradivarius." Stringer, a reputable antique dealer, made no positive representations to that effect, however, and Player relied on his own judgment in the matter. Accordingly, Player paid Stringer $250,000 and received the violin. At the time of the purchase, Stringer also handed Player a "bill of sale" disclaiming, under applicable provisions of the Uniform Commercial Code, all express or implied warranties. The "bill of sale" was signed by Stringer but not by Player.

A short time later, Player discovered that the violin that he purchased was not an original Stradivarius but a masterful imitation. The violin was valued at only $300.

3. Player now brings an appropriate action against Stringer to rescind the contract and recover the $250,000. Which of the following will the court probably decide?

    (A) Stringer will win, because the sales contract was valid and enforceable under the doctrine of caveat emptor.
    (B) Stringer will win, because the "bill of sale" disclaimed any warranties as to the genuineness of the violin.
    (C) Player will win, because although the sales contract was valid, it would be unenforceable under the Statute of Frauds since Player did not sign the "bill of sale."
    (D) Player will win, because although the sales contract was valid, it would be voidable by Player since the parties were mutually mistaken about the genuineness of the violin.

Question 4 refers to the following fact pattern.

Dee Sario had failed the California bar exam three times. On her fourth try, she hired a tutor, Cheri Carney, to help prepare her for the next exam. The parties formalized a written contract in which Cheri promised to tutor Dee for four weeks and Dee promised to pay Cheri $5,000 for her services. At the time the women entered into their agreement, Dee orally promised to pay Cheri an additional $1,000 if she was successful on the bar exam.

4. Assume that Cheri tutored Dee for two weeks when Dee suddenly died from a brain tumor. Cheri made a written demand to Dee's estate seeking payment for services rendered. After the executor of Dee's estate refused to authorize such payment, Cheri filed a contract action against Dee's estate. Cheri should

    (A) recover nothing, because the estate was not unjustly enriched.
    (B) recover nothing, because of impossibility of performance.
    (C) recover quantum meruit, for the reasonable value of services rendered.
    (D) recover $2,500, or the equivalent of one half of the stipulated contract amount.

Question 5 refers to the following fact pattern.

Maxwell owned a men's haberdashery in Chicago. In anticipation of a cold winter, Maxwell wanted to have a large quantity of scarves in stock for his customers. Maxwell telephoned Scarface, a scarf wholesaler, and ordered 600 scarves for October 1 delivery. Scarface promised to deliver 600 scarves at the agreed price of $10 per scarf.

Thereafter, Scarface did an inventory and learned that he only had 550 scarves in stock. Without notifying Maxwell, Scarface went ahead and delivered the 550 scarves to Maxwell on October 1. When Maxwell learned that the shipment contained 550 scarves instead of 600, he refused to accept delivery and did not make any payment.

5. If Maxwell brings suit against Scarface for breach of contract, what damages, if any, will he be entitled to?

    (A) None, because the agreement was unenforceable under the Statute of Frauds.
    (B) The contract price minus the cost of replacement.
    (C) $6,000.
    (D) $5,500.

Question 6 refers to the following fact pattern.

Breeder owned a kennel where he bred Old English sheepdogs. On March 15, Breeder and Buyer entered into a written agreement wherein Breeder promised to sell Buyer a sheepdog puppy for $500. Under the terms of the contract, Breeder promised to deliver the dog to Buyer on April 15, and Buyer agreed to pay Breeder $250 on June 1 and $250 on October 1.

On April 15 Breeder did deliver a sheepdog puppy to Buyer, which he accepted. Buyer, however, failed to make the June 1 payment when it came due. On June 1 the puppy that Breeder delivered to Buyer had a market value of $600.

6. Having not received the June 1st payment, Breeder sues Buyer for breach of contract on June 5th. What is the maximum amount of general damages that Breeder can recover?

    (A) Nothing, because Breeder must wait until October 1st before bringing suit.
    (B) $250 for the partial breach that has occurred.
    (C) $500 for breach of the entire contract.
    (D) $600, because Buyer would be unjustly enriched by that amount.

Question 7 refers to the following fact pattern.

Applegate, a wholesaler of Washington state apples, entered into a written contract to supply Gelson's, a California supermarket, with 20 bushels of red Fuji variety apples. The contract provided that Gelson's would pay $20 per bushel, and Applegate contracted with Coastal Transport Company, a west coast cargo service, to have them deliver the apples to Gelson's warehouse in California. Applegate, in turn, packaged the 20 bushels of apples and gave them to Coastal with shipping instructions for delivery to Gelson's. Coastal placed the apples on its cargo plane for an overnight flight to California. During the airflight the plane experienced mechanical difficulty and crashed. A subsequent investigation revealed that the crash was due to negligence on the part of the Coastal pilot. As a result of the airplane crash, the apples were destroyed.

7. Assume that Gelson's had other distributors supplying the Fuji apples. After the airline crash, Gelson's contracted with Martindale, another apple wholesaler, and purchased 20 bushels of the same Fuji apples for $390. The standard market value for the 20 bushels of Fuji apples was $450. If Gelson's sues Applegate for breach, what, if anything, is Gelson's measure of recovery?

   (A) Nothing
   (B) $10
   (C) $50
   (D) $60

Question 8 refers to the following fact pattern.

Norma Nameth was an 80-year-old widow who was confined to a wheelchair after undergoing a hip replacement operation. Norma lived in West Grove, a remote rural town ninety miles west of Philadelphia. Since Norma was unable to walk, her son, Nellie decided to hire a home health care worker to cook and look after his mother. Thereupon, Nellie entered into an oral agreement with Goldie Goodfellow, a certified health care worker, to serve as a live-in companion for his ailing mother.

According to their agreement, Goldie would provide live-in care for Norma six days a week from Monday through Saturday with Sunday designated as her day off.

The parties further agreed that Nellie would pay Goldie $600 per week and that Goldie would serve as a health care worker for a ten-month period.

Goldie started to care for Norma on February 1 and worked continuously until July 1 when she gave notice that she would be quitting. Thereafter, Nellie learned that Goldie had been hired away by Inca Inkster, Norma's invalid neighbor, who agreed to pay Goldie $800 per week to care for her.

Nellie then attempted to hire another home health care worker to care for Norma. However, no other companions were available because of the remote locale of Norma's home.

8. Nellie brings suit seeking to enforce his employment agreement with Goldie and enjoin her from working for Inca. Nellie should

   (A) lose, because his employment agreement with Goldie was oral, it would be unenforceable under the Statute of Frauds.
   (B) lose, because requiring Goldie to work against her will would be a form of involuntary servitude.
   (C) lose, because his proper cause of action should be for money damages.
   (D) win, because Goldie has committed a material breach of contract and may be enjoined from working for Inca.

Question 9 refers to the following fact pattern.

Autry and Biggerstaff are adjoining homeowners in a residential neighborhood. Autry begins to operate a slaughterhouse in his backyard. The putrid smell from the slaughterhouse travels over Biggerstaff's property. Biggerstaff and his family members find the odor to be foul and nauseating. As a result of Autry's slaughterhouse, Biggerstaff's property value has diminished 20%. There is no applicable zoning ordinance preventing Autry's slaughterhouse operation.

9. Biggerstaff has asserted a nuisance action against Autry. The complaint seeks recovery for damages and injunctive relief enjoining operation of the slaughterhouse. The court should

    (A) award damages but not grant injunctive relief.
    (B) grant injunctive relief but not award damages.
    (C) grant injunctive relief and award damages.
    (D) neither award damages nor grant injunctive relief because there was no violation of any ordinance.

Question 10 refers to the following fact pattern.

Neptune Aeronautics was in the business of launching communication satellites for private commercial uses. In anticipation of being awarded a government license to establish a new communication radio frequency spectrum, Neptune entered into contract with Solar Systems Inc. The agreement called for Solar Systems to design and develop unique communications satellite in accord with plans and specifications supplied by Neptune.

Neptune informed Solar Systems that until the government contract was actually awarded, it could not provide Solar Systems with all the specifications required to complete the construction of the satellite. Nevertheless, Neptune was confident that the license would be awarded and expressly agreed to assume the risk that it would receive final contract approval from the government. Under the terms of the agreement, Neptune agreed to pay Solar Systems $3,000,000 upon completion of the satellite.

Solar Systems then began working on the satellite project and spent $1,000,000 in developmental costs. Afterwards, the government decided not to pursue the satellite project and informed Neptune that it would not be receiving any authorization or licensing for the satellite. Neptune immediately contacted Solar Systems and cancelled its contract. Thereupon, Solar Systems discontinued any further work on the satellite.

10. Solar Systems has filed suit for breach of contract against Neptune. Assume for the purposes of this question that it would be impossible for either party to determine the market value for such a unique satellite (given the lack of governmental specifications). Moreover, neither party can establish with reasonable certainty the completion cost for the satellite. If Neptune is found liable for breach, Solar Systems should be entitled to recover

    (A) $1,000,000, in reliance damages.
    (B) $1,000,000, as restitutionary damages.
    (C) $1,000,000, plus incidental damages.
    (D) $3,000,000, the contract price because Neptune assumed the risk of not being awarded the government license.

Question 11 refers to the following fact pattern.

Ohner wanted to have a security system installed in his home. He contacted several companies and asked them to submit bids for the installation work. One of them, Alarmco, in turn, requested bids from several wholesalers for the burglar alarms it planned to use if it was awarded the job. Supplier submitted a bid to Alarmco that the latter used in computing the bid that it was preparing for Ohner.

On September 1, Alarmco sent Ohner its bid in which it proposed to install the security system for $12,000. On September 9, Supplier notified Alarmco that it would be unable to supply any burglar alarms to them. On September 11, Ohner sent the following telegram to Alarmco, "I hereby accept your offer to install the security system for $12,000."

Alarmco had to pay another wholesaler $3,000 above the price quoted by Supplier for the burglar alarms. As a result, Alarmco advised Ohner that the total price for the job would have to be increased to $15,000. Ohner replied that he would hold Alarmco to the initially agreed price of $12,000. Alarmco went ahead and installed the security system, but Ohner has not yet paid them anything.

11. In an action by Alarmco against Ohner for services rendered, Alarmco will probably be able to recover

    (A) $12,000, because that was the contract price.
    (B) $15,000, because of an unanticipated change of circumstances after the parties had entered into their contract.
    (C) only in quantum meruit, because of the doctrine of commercial frustration.
    (D) only in quantum meruit, because by demanding $15,000 Alarmco repudiated its contract with Ohner.

Question 12 refers to the following fact pattern.

Morgana, a 25-year-old concert pianist, lived in a small studio apartment on West 52nd Street in New York City. Morgana couldn't keep a piano in her apartment because of its small dimensions. In order to practice each day, she had to travel to the Julliard School of Performing Arts to use their musical facilities. Finally, Morgana decided to move out of her apartment and buy a more spacious home where she could have her own piano. As she was house hunting, Morgana found a quaint Cape Cod style home in Westchester that she wanted. She put a bid down on the home with the seller's broker. But she was informed that the owner was in Europe on a business trip and would not be entertaining any offers until he returned.

While she was awaiting word on the Westchester property, Morgana's friend, Tito, orally agreed to sell his Baldwin Baby Grand to her for $8,000. Morgana explained that she wanted the piano only if she should succeed in her efforts to buy the Westchester home. For this reason, the parties agreed that the piano sale would not take effect "unless Morgana buys the Westchester home." The next day, the parties reduced their oral agreement to a signed writing.

12. Assume Morgana did, in fact, purchase the Cape Cod home in Westchester. Thereupon, she tendered a $8,000 cashier's check to Tito for the Baldwin piano. Tito rejected the tender and refused to deliver the piano to Morgana. If Morgana brings an action for breach of contract against Tito, Morgana is entitled to which of the following remedies?

    I. Damages measured by the difference between the market price and the contract price for the piano.
    II. Recovery of the contract price of the piano.
    III. Specific performance.

    (A) I only.
    (B) II only.
    (C) I or III, at Morgana's election.
    (D) II or III, at Morgana's election.

Question 13 refers to the following fact pattern.

National Widget Company, whose principal business office is located in Ft. Worth, Texas, is engaged in the retail sale of widgets throughout the United States. McCormick Equipment Corporation is the nation's largest manufacturer and wholesaler of widgets. McCormick's corporate headquarters are located in Nashville, Tennessee. On March 7, 2003, Johnny Lee, President of National, sent McCormick the following purchase order:

> "Promptly ship 1,000 widgets, catalogue #B4-IEU, at the current wholesale price to our Ft. Worth office. Thank you for your attention to this matter.
>
> /s/ Lee"

This order was received by McCormick on March 9. The next day, McCormick replied by telegram:

> "Your order has been received. Shipment date will be March 12. Price $50 for each widget delivered. Be advised that these are the last widgets, under catalogue #B4-IEU, that we can deliver since this variety is no longer being manufactured."

This telegram was received by Lee on March 11. He immediately telegraphed McCormick:

> "Cancel our previous order for 1,000 widgets under catalogue #B4-IEU. Price too high."

McCormick received this telegram on March 11. On March 13, McCormick sold the 1,000 widgets, catalogue #B4-IEU, to Western Widgetry, another retail widget company in Dallas, for $50 each, which was the current wholesale market price.

13. Assume for the purposes of this question only that a contract was in fact formed between National and McCormick. In an action for breach of contract by McCormick against National, what is the maximum amount of damages that McCormick should be entitled to recover?

    (A) Nothing.
    (B) Only the incidental damages, if any, that McCormick has incurred in preparing the widgets for shipment to National before receiving National's telegram of March 11.
    (C) $50,000, or the price of $50 per widget as ordered.
    (D) Consequential damages since these widgets were unique due to the fact that they were the last of its kind to be manufactured.

Question 14 refers to the following fact pattern.

On April 18, 2001, Vito, an owner of a vending machine business, mailed a purchase order requesting immediate shipment to Medford Dairy Company for 400 gal. of milk at $1 per gallon.

On April 23, Vito was informed that many of his machines had been damaged by vandalism. As a result, Vito promptly called the manager of Medford Diary and requested that his purchase order be canceled. The manager replied that he could not do so, since the milk delivery was already in transit. Moreover the manager told Vito that it would be impossible for him to cancel the order, because he had just made commitments with several farmers to purchase additional milk. When the shipment arrived, Vito refused to accept it. Medford was then forced to sell the milk elsewhere at a loss of $150. Medford demanded reimbursement of their loss on the resale of the milk.

14. In an action by Medford Dairy Co. against Vito demanding reimbursement for its loss of $150 on the resale of the milk, judgment for

    (A) Medford, since their appropriate remedy would be to "cover."
    (B) Medford, since their acceptance of Vito's purchase order created an enforceable contract.
    (C) Vito, since frustration of purpose would relieve him of liability.
    (D) Vito, since under the circumstances, the revocation of his acceptance would be effective.

Question 15 refers to the following fact pattern.

Dexter, a collector of vintage automobiles, became friendly with Arthur, a young antique dealer. One evening Arthur told Dexter that Oscar owned a collection of Persian rugs valued at $100,000, which he believed that they could purchase for $50,000. Arthur had $5,000 in cash and owned a Rolls Royce, which was valued at $50,000.

After many discussions, Arthur and Dexter entered into the following agreement:

"July 16, 2008

Upon Arthur's request, at any time within one year from the date hereof, Dexter will lend Arthur $50,000 without interest, at which time Arthur will deliver his 1945 Rolls Royce to Dexter. The money will be repayable to Dexter one year from the date. If Arthur is unable to repay the $50,000 at the end of the year, Dexter will sell the Rolls Royce. Dexter will then retain $50,000 of the proceeds and give the rest to Arthur. If Dexter sells the Rolls Royce for less than $50,000, Arthur will pay Dexter the difference.

(signed) Arthur

(signed) Dexter"

The next day Arthur and Dexter executed the following written agreement:

"July 17, 2008

In consideration of friendship and affection, I desire to give Dexter an interest in the Persian rugs which I plan to purchase from Oscar and then resell through Perry, a Persian rug dealer. in the event I receive over $100,000 from the sale, I will I give Dexter 30% of the excess.

(signed) Arthur

Accepted

(signed) Dexter"

Thereafter, Arthur attempted to purchase the rugs from Oscar. Finally in February 2009, Oscar agreed to sell the rugs to Arthur for $60,000. Arthur then came to Dexter with his Rolls Royce and requested the $50,000 loan immediately. Dexter, who had lost interest in the transaction, refused to lend Arthur any money.

As a consequence, on February 15, 1980, Arthur borrowed $50,000 at 11% interest from the Wells Fargo Bank and purchased the rugs for $60,000 on that day. On April 1, 2009, Arthur sold the rugs to Perry for $150,000. When Dexter learned of the sale, he contacted Arthur and demanded $15,000. Arthur refused to turn over any of the proceeds from the sale to Dexter and, in turn, demanded that Dexter pay him $5,500, the amount of interest due on his Wells Fargo loan.

15. In an action by Arthur to recover the $5,500 against Dexter for breach of contract, he will most likely

    (A) succeed, since Dexter's refusal to perform constituted an anticipatory repudiation.
    (B) succeed, since Arthur would be entitled to recover compensatory damages for Dexter's non-performance.
    (C) not succeed, since the July 16th agreement was unenforceable as a matter of law.
    (D) not succeed, since Dexter's contractual obligations under the July 16th agreement would be discharged by novation.

Question 16 refers to the following fact pattern.

Ohner owned a large three-story office building in downtown Metropolis. She planned to renovate the building and requested several contractors to submit bids to perform the work. One of the contractors, Builder, in turn sought bids from several subcontractors to determine the overall cost of the job. Electrician submitted a bid to Builder that he used in computing the bid he sent to Ohner. Builder notified Electrician to that effect.

On November 1, Builder submitted his bid to Ohner in which he offered to perform the renovation work for $75,000. On November 4, Electrician notified Builder that he was unable to perform the electrical work on Ohner's project. On November 5, Ohner sent Builder a signed confirmation letter wherein she stated, "I hereby accept your offer to perform the renovation work for the quoted cost of $75,000." Thereafter, Builder hired another electrician to complete the electrical work at a cost of $5,000 above Electrician's bid. Builder explained the situation to Ohner and informed her that the overall cost of the job would have to be increased to $80,000. Ohner responded that she would hold Builder to his original bid of $75,000 and would not be responsible for any additional costs. Builder then performed the renovation work, but Ohner has not yet paid him anything.

16. In an action by Builder against Ohner for the services rendered, Builder will probably be able to recover

    (A) only in *quantum meruit*, because of the doctrine of commercial frustration.
    (B) only in *quantum meruit*, because by demanding $80,000 Builder, in effect, repudiated his contract with Ohner.
    (C) $75,000 only, because that was the contract price.
    (D) $80,000, because Builder reasonably relied to his detriment on Electrician's bid in formulating his job estimate.

Questions 17 and 18 refer to the following fact pattern.

On April 10, Gallop, owner of the Galloping Hill Golf Course in Unionville, entered into an oral agreement with Sprink. Based upon their agreement, Sprink promised to install all new sprinkler heads on the sprinkler system at the eighteen-hole golf course. In return, Gallop promised to pay Sprink $2,400 upon completion of the job. Since the Unionville County Golf Tournament was scheduled for the weekend of April 20-21, Sprink agreed to replace all the sprinkler heads no later than April 19. Before accepting the job, Sprink had inspected the golf course and determined that 240 sprinkler heads had to be replaced.

By April 14, Sprink had installed eighty new sprinkler heads on the first six holes of the eighteen-hole golf course. That afternoon, however, Gallop learned that Sprink had been adjudicated bankrupt on April 12. So, therefore, Gallop notified Sprink to discontinue the job. The next day, Gallop hired Hand to complete the installation work at eight dollars ($8) per head. Hand installed the remaining one hundred sixty sprinkler heads and completed the work on April 19. Despite making reasonable efforts, Sprink was unable to find any gainful employment during the period that Hand completed the job. Also, Sprink's application for unemployment compensation was rejected at the same time.

17. Assume for the purposes of this question only that Gallop was legally justified in discharging Sprink. In an action by Sprink against Gallop, which of the following is Sprink's proper measure of recovery?

    (A) $640 (or the equivalent of $8 per sprinkler head installed).
    (B) $800 (or the equivalent of $10 per sprinkler head installed).
    (C) Quantum meruit for the reasonable value of his services rendered in installing the eighty sprinkler heads.
    (D) Nothing, because he has not completed performance of the entire job.

18. Assume for the purposes of this question only that Gallop was not legally justified in discharging Sprink. In an action by Sprink against Gallop, which of the following is Sprink's proper measure of recovery?

    (A) $2,400, less the savings he effects by not completing the job.
    (B) $2,080 (or the equivalent of the total contract price of $2,400 minus $320 that Gallop saved by employing Hand).
    (C) $1,120 (or the equivalent of the contract unit price for the sprinklers that Sprink installed plus the $320 that Gallop saved by employing Hand).
    (D) $800 (or the equivalent of the contract unit price for the sprinklers that Sprink installed).

Question 19 refers to the following fact pattern.

On March 1, 2003 Ohner, entered into a written contract with Contractor wherein the latter agreed to remodel the basement of Ohner's house for $20,000. According to the terms of the agreement, Ohner promised to pay Contractor $10,000 on May 1, 2003, when work was to commence with the balance payable upon completion of the job.

On April 1, 2003, Contractor sent Ohner a letter stating that the cost of building materials had increased from his original estimate. Consequently, Contractor indicated that he didn't think he could perform the remodeling work unless Ohner agreed to increase the price to $25,000. Without notifying Contractor, Ohner went ahead and hired Carpenter to perform the remodeling for the price of $22,000, which was the fair market cost of the work to be done.

Carpenter started renovating the basement on April 26, 2003. On May 1, 2003, Contractor showed up at Ohner's home. Contractor told Ohner he reconsidered and was ready to begin remodeling the basement at the original contract price. Ohner then informed him that he had hired someone else and dismissed Contractor from the job.

19. Assume that Contractor is liable for repudiating the contract. In addition, assume that Carpenter completed the remodeling of the basement at a cost of $30,000. Ohner went ahead and paid Carpenter the contract price of $22,000 plus the additional $8,000 so that Carpenter wouldn't lose any money. In a breach of contract action by Ohner against Contractor, Ohner should recover

    (A) $2,000, or the difference between Contractor's contract price and Carpenter's contract price.
    (B) $5,000, or the difference between Contractor's original contract price and the amount he demanded in his April 1st letter.
    (C) $10,000, or the difference between Contractor's original contract price and the amount Ohner paid Carpenter.
    (D) the difference between the fair market value of the completed remodeling work and Contractor's original contract price.

Question 20 refers to the following fact pattern.

The states of Concord and Kent have as a common border the Delaware River. The highway departments of the two states prepared plans for an interstate highway that would cross the Delaware River. On March 15, 2002, the highway department of the state of Concord and Valvano Construction Co. signed a written contract by which Valvano undertook to build a bridge with a four-lane highway from the Concord shoreline to the middle of the Delaware River, in accordance with specifications supplied by the Concord Highway Department.

The contract price was $600,000 of which $300,000 was to be paid when the ten piers called for by the specifications were completed, $200,000 when the connecting superstructure was completed, and $100,000 when the roadway was completed and ready for use. Valvano undertook to complete the whole job by December 1, 2003. In addition, the contract contained the following provisions:

> "5. The bridge is to be operated as a toll bridge, and delay in completion will cause inconvenience to the public, loss of revenue and interest on investment, and administrative expenses. To cover partially such losses and expenses the Contractor (Valvano) will pay the State of Concord as liquidated damages the sum of $1,000 for each day's delay in completion.
>
> 6. The Concord Highway Department has made and does make no representations as to the condition of the subsoil beneath the Delaware River, which is entirely at the risk of the Contractor."

Two weeks later, on April 1, 2002, the Concord Highway Department entered into a contract with a road builder to build a four-lane highway, fifteen miles long, from the Concord state Capitol to connect with the bridge over the Delaware. This work was started immediately and finally completed in September 2003, at which time the road builder was paid the contract price of $240,000.

However, Valvano, the owner of the construction company, ran into difficulties from the outset. His workmen struck for two months and he was forced to increase their wages by 25%. His investigation of the subsoil had been inadequate, and he discovered that at the sites of four of the piers the subsoil was heavy clay that required extensive dynamiting. Under two other piers, loose gravel extending down 125 feet required much deeper excavation than anticipated. The ten piers were finally completed by October 1, 2003, and on October 7, 2003, the Concord Highway Department paid Valvano $300,000.

At an election in the state of Kent on November 6, 2003, a statewide referendum on a proposed bond issue for highway construction was defeated by a large margin. The Kent state highway department on November 13, 2003 announced that it had run out of funds. It had earlier contracted with another contractor to build the Kent half of the bridge over the Delaware but progress on this job had been even slower than that of Valvano. On November 24, 2003, the Kent Highway Department terminated this contract, paid indemnity to the contractor, and abandoned any effort to finish the bridge.

On December 1, 2003, the Concord Highway Department notified Valvano that he was already more than 150 days behind schedule, that under the liquidated damage clause he would be liable for at least $150,000 and that the highway department would not under any circumstances make any further payments to Valvano.

Thereupon, Valvano consulted with his engineers who have advised him that they were more than 150 days behind schedule and that even with overtime and a resulting 30% increase in costs, it would take at least 100 days to complete the bridge. Valvano, who has already spent $550,000 on the job, has estimated that it would cost another $280,000 to complete it, and within two weeks he will run out of funds to pay his workmen and suppliers.

20. Which of the following is the most accurate statement regarding the enforcement of the liquidation of damages clause?

    (A) The clause is likely to be enforceable because parties to a contract may effectively provide in advance the damages that are to be payable in the event of breach as long as the provision does not disregard the principle of compensation.
    (B) The clause is likely to be enforceable because the amount of $1,000 per day is reasonable in light of the anticipated or actual loss caused by the breach and the difficulties of proof of loss.
    (C) The clause is likely to be unenforceable because the amount of $1,000 per day is so unreasonably large as to be a penalty.
    (D) The clause is likely to be unenforceable because Valvano's delay in completing the bridge has not caused the Concord Highway Department any loss due to the fact that Kent has discontinued work on its section of the bridge.

Question 21 refers to the following fact pattern.

On May 1, 1993, Irving borrowed $5,000 interest-free from his brother-in-law, Harry. Under the terms of the promissory note, Irving promised to repay the debt upon demand. On March 1, 1997, Harry contacted Irving and requested repayment of the debt. Irving, who was unemployed at the time, notified Harry that he did not have sufficient funds to pay any of the debt. Harry did not make any further demands upon Irving with regard to the loan. The statute of limitations for such debt obligations is ten years in this jurisdiction.

On June 1, 2003, Irving was still without any funds to repay the debt. Although he was aware that the debt was barred by the statute of limitations, he felt guilty that he was unable to repay at least part of the loan. As a result, Irving approached his friend, Joel, and asked him if he would be willing to pay Harry $600 on his behalf. Joel agreed but he asked Irving, "Well, what do I get out of this?" Irving told Joel that he was broke. However, Irving said, "All right, Joel, I know you've always wanted my Bruce Springsteen T-shirt." Joel orally accepted Irving's offer and took the T-shirt.

On August 1, 2003, Irving telephoned Joel and asked if he had paid Harry the $600. Joel said that he had changed his mind and decided not to pay Harry anything. Joel also told Irving that he was going to keep the T-shirt. On July 4, 2003, Harry became aware of Joel's promise to Irving.

21. Suppose that Irving sues Joel for breach of contract, which of the following is correct?

    (A) Joel would prevail because the monetary value of his oral promise to Irving exceeded $500.
    (B) Except for nominal damages, Joel will prevail because Irving did not suffer any damage from Joel's breach of promise.
    (C) Irving would be entitled to recover $600 from Joel for his breach of promise.
    (D) Irving would be entitled to specific performance of Joel's promise.

Question 22 refers to the following fact pattern.

On October 1, 1974, Jackson Stone, owner of several hundred acres in the County of Los Angeles, drafted a general development plan for the area, to be known as the Del Mar addition. The duly recorded plan imposed elaborate limitations and restrictions upon the land in the addition, which was to be developed as a residence district. The restrictions were to extend to all persons acquiring any of the lots and to their heirs, assigns, and lessees. It was further provided that all subsequent owners would be charged with due notice of the restrictions.

Among those restrictions in the general plan were the following:

(A) A franchise right is created in a strip of land ten feet in width along the rear of each lot for the use of public utility companies with right of ingress and egress.

(B) No house or structure of any kind shall be built on the aforementioned strip of land running through the said blocks.

In 1994, Bernie Smith purchased one of the lots, built a house, and erected a fence in the rear of his property within the restricted area. In 1998, Wilber Hemmings purchased a lot adjacent to the Smith property and built a new house. Two years later, Sam Roberts purchased the lot that adjoined Wilber's property. The three deeds to those properties each contained references to the deed-book where the general plan was recorded.

In 2002, Sam Roberts began the construction of a seven-foot post-and-rail fence along the line dividing his lot with Wilber's and along the center of the area subject to the franchise right. Although Wilber objected to its construction, the fence was completed.

22. If Wilber seeks a mandatory injunction to compel removal of Sam Robert's fence, the court will most likely

    (A) grant relief, since the fence was in violation of the easement restriction.
    (B) grant relief, since the encroachment of the fence violated the restriction in the original plan.
    (C) deny relief, since Wilber failed to enforce the restriction against Bernie Smith.
    (D) deny relief, since the fence would not be construed as "a structure" within the terms of the restriction.

Questions 23 and 24 refer to the following fact pattern.

The General Services Administration (GSA) of the state government advertised for bids from general contractors on construction of a state office building of specified dimensions. George, who intended to submit a bid to GSA on the project, solicited bids from various subcontractors for framing, electrical work, plumbing, etc. George subsequently received a sub-bid on the plumbing work for the project of $510,000 from Peter, a plumbing subcontractor. Peter's bid was $10,000 lower than any competing sub-bid. After compiling all the acceptable sub-bids, George submitted a bid to GSA on the total project for $5 million. This was the lowest bid submitted to GSA, which accepted George's bid on that basis. That same day, George notified Peter that his plumbing sub-bid was accepted.

A week after GSA accepted George's bid, Peter notified George that an accounting error had resulted in his plumbing sub-bid being too low by $50,000; the actual bid should have been $560,000 for the plumbing work.

23. If Peter brings an appropriate action to rescind his contract with George for the plumbing work on the GSA project, judgment should be for:

    (A) Peter, because the error deprives him of the benefit of the bargain of his contract.
    (B) Peter, because his unilateral mistake deprives the parties of the mutual assent necessary for formation of a contract.
    (C) George, because he was unaware of Peter's mistake and had no reason to know of it.
    (D) George, because a unilateral mistake can never be the basis for rescission.

24. Assume for purposes of this question only that Peter had transmitted his sub-bid to George via telegraph, and that the telegraph company's error in transmission caused the bid to read "$360,000" instead of the accurate "$560,000." All other facts are as previously set forth. Which of the following is Peter's strongest argument for rescission?

    (A) George's negligence in not verifying the accuracy of all sub-bids precludes enforcement of the contract.
    (B) George should have known that Peter's sub-bid was erroneous because it was $160,000 lower than any other plumbing sub-bid.
    (C) George has an adequate remedy against the real wrongdoer—the telegraph company.
    (D) The fact that Peter was forced to submit his sub-bid before George submitted the main bid to GSA demonstrates that the George-Peter agreement was an adhesion contract.

Question 25 refers to the following fact pattern.

After his female rottweiler, Himtodt's Lustig Lady, had won her fifth consecutive Best in Show at the annual, world-renowned Metropolis Kennel Club Dog Show, Himtodt was approached by a number of people interested in puppies from Lady (her call name). Pursued most ardently by Clavin, Himtodt jotted down the following on a blank piece of paper: "Clavin shall be entitled to purchase the 'pick of the litter' from each of the next three litters born by Himtodt's Lustig Lady. Pup to be selected no earlier than eight weeks of age and no later than twelve weeks of age. Price to be determined by conformation at time of selection." Both Himtodt and Clavin signed the writing, and Clavin took possession of it.

Lady's next litter was whelped five months later. When the pups were nine weeks of age, Clavin appeared at Himtodt's kennel, examined the litter, selected a pup, and presented Himtodt with a check for $3,000. Pups from litters of other champion Rottweilers ranged in cost at that time from $500 to $2,500 dollars. Himtodt refused to sell the pup for less than $10,000. Clavin immediately brought an appropriate action to determine the parties' rights and remedies in this matter.

25. Assume that a completely enforceable contract existed between the parties for the sale of a pup, and that Himtodt's refusal to deliver the selected pup for $3,000 is a breach of that agreement, to what relief is Clavin entitled?

    (A) $3,000, the contract price.
    (B) The difference between the contract price and the cost of obtaining a comparable pup, at least $500.
    (C) Specific performance of the contract.
    (D) Specific performance of the contract or $3,000, the contract price, at his election.

Questions 26 and 27 refer to the following fact pattern.

Through an inadvertent governmental leak, Beau learned that testing by the Food and Drug Administration seemed to indicate that a compound used in the aging of Gouda cheese caused cancer when ingested by laboratory mice. The test results were due to be officially released in nine months. Beau, the president of a domestic Gouda cheese producer, contacted Samuel. Samuel was a leading organic chemist specializing in the development of dairy-related procedures and products. Samuel claimed to have developed a new compound which he referred to as "Agee" that would replace the compound presently used. Beau contracted in writing with Samuel to purchase 1,000 pounds of Agee at $10 per pound, freight prepaid to Beau's plant.

Beau realized that purchasers of his cheese would demand the same mild flavored, close-textured cheese that is characteristic of Gouda cheese. Therefore, the contract of sale expressly provided that the use of Agee would not impact the generally recognized character of the cheese. The contract also provided that the Agee would be delivered in lots of 250 pounds per month beginning June 1, that Beau should pay for each lot of 250 pounds as delivered, and that Beau would make payment within 24 hours after delivery.

Immediately upon delivery of the first lot of 250 pounds of Agee on June 1, Beau forwarded to Samuel a check for $2,500. Upon testing the Agee, Beau determined that its use was likely to result in a considerably sharper cheese. Proper testing of the Agee required at least 72 hours and cost Beau $2,500. Beau decided that, despite the test results, he would use 50 pounds of Agee in actual production of the cheese. On June 25, Beau notified Samuel that he was rejecting all of the Agee delivered and would reject all future deliveries because of the changes to the character of the cheese that resulted when Agee was used.

26. With respect to the 200 pounds delivered but unused Agee assuming Beau's rejection of the Agee was justified, Beau can recover:

    (A) Nothing.
    (B) Two-thirds of the $2,000 he paid for it.
    (C) The entire $2,000, and he can resell the Agee for Samuel's account.
    (D) The entire $2,000 he paid for them, but he cannot resell the Agee for Samuel's account.

27. In addition to recovery, if any, on the 200 pounds delivered but unused Agee, Beau can also recover:

    (A) Punitive damages for an additional $2,000.
    (B) Inspection costs plus any costs for the care and custody of the Agee.
    (C) The amount he can prove he lost due to the delay in placing his Gouda cheese on the market.
    (D) Damages for his mental suffering.

Question 28 refers to the following fact pattern.

Like millions of other Americans, Bueller was anxious to purchase one of the new Mitsusushi two-way wrist videophones, the Walk-'n-Talkman. He went to the Electron Store, a chain retailer of consumer electronic devices, to purchase one. The Electron Store paid $1,500 to the factory for the Walk-'n-Talkman and charged its customers $2,500. Although each Walk-'n-Talkman had to be preordered from the factory, Electron Store could obtain a Walk-'n-Talkman for any order it received. An Electron Store salesperson filled out a preprinted form which had been drafted by the Electron Store's corporate legal department, in which Bueller agreed to make a $300 down payment and to pay the remaining $2,200 upon delivery of the Walk-'n-Talkman to him. Bueller signed the form without reading it.

When Bueller's Walk-'n-Talkman arrived from Japan six weeks later, Bueller refused to accept it and demanded his $300 down payment back. The Electron Store immediately sold that Walk-'n-Talkman for $2,500 to Calistoga, who had also ordered one from the factory on the same terms as Bueller. The Electron Store then brought an action for breach of contract against Bueller, who counterclaimed for return of his $300.

28. What will be the likely outcome of this action?

    (A) Judgment for Bueller in the amount of $300, because the purchase agreement was an unconscionable adhesion contract.
    (B) Judgment for the Electron Store for the incidental costs of sale, since it resold the Walk-'n-Talkman at no loss to itself.
    (C) Judgment for the Electron Store in the amount of $700 plus reasonable overhead and incidental costs, because under the circumstances, loss of profit is the only measure of damages which will make the Electron Store whole.
    (D) Judgment for the Electron Store in the amount of $2,200, because it could sell every Walk-'n-Talkman it could obtain from the factory.

Question 29 refers to the following fact pattern.

Contractor agreed to build a restaurant for Developer in accordance with detailed plans and specifications. In return, Developer agreed to pay Contractor $100,000 for the restaurant upon completion. The written contract included the following provision: "Developer's liability is expressly conditioned on use of South African rose marble to floor the foyer." Thereafter, Developer contracted in writing to sell the restaurant to Businessman, and the Developer-Businessman written contract contained the following provision: "This contract is contingent upon Businessman obtaining financing at 10 percent interest." While the restaurant was under construction, the President of the United States, acting under proper legal authorization, banned all further trade with South Africa. Since no South African rose marble was otherwise available, Contractor used a similar fine quality Italian marble in the foyer instead.

Businessman attempted to procure a loan from several institutions, but found that he could not obtain financing at 10 percent due to a slump in the real estate market and his "spotty" credit history.

Sub had agreed in writing with Contractor to paper the walls in a Belgian string wall covering. Unfortunately, Sub used two different dye lots, and the paper did not quite match, although it was otherwise functional.

Other than the floor and wall covering, the restaurant was completed according to the plans and specifications contained in the Contractor-Developer contract.

29. If Developer refused to pay Contractor on the ground that the wall covering does not match, which of the following is the most likely result?

    (A) Developer must pay the contract price minus the diminished value of the restaurant because of the defective wall covering.
    (B) Developer must pay the full contract price without any offset for the defective wall covering because Contractor substantially performed.
    (C) Developer must pay Contractor the full contract price because any damages resulting from the defective wall covering are recoverable only from the Sub.
    (D) Developer is not required to pay Contractor anything until the defect in the wall's covering is completely remedied.

Question 30 refers to the following fact pattern.

30. Lawyer was overjoyed when he received the announcement from the Committee of Bar Exam-iners declaring that he had passed. However, he was even more pleased when the firm of Good, Better & Best ("Firm") offered him an associate position. On December 1, Lawyer signed the written one-year employment contract with Firm. The contract provided for a $48,000 salary, with the one-year term commencing January 1.

    Assume that on January 1 Lawyer failed to appear for work because he had accepted an associate position with Prestige, Prominence & Profitable. Without inquiring why Lawyer failed to report for work, Firm hired Associate, the only available substitute, to fill the position for the month of January at a salary of $4,500, the amount that Associate demanded.

    On January 31, after learning why Lawyer had not reported on January 1, Firm hired Associate to fill the position for the next 11 months at a total salary of $54,000, payable $4,500 per month. If Firm sues Lawyer on February 1, how much is Firm entitled to recover, assuming judgment is rendered on February 28?

    (A) $500 in damages for January.
    (B) $1,000 in damages for January and February.
    (C) $1,000 in damages for January and February plus the discounted present value of the $500 salary differentials for the months of March through December.
    (D) Nothing, because Firm did not attempt to contact Lawyer on January 1 to ascertain why he failed to appear for work.

Question 31 refers to the following fact pattern.

Ostek owned a vacant lot upon which he wished to operate a gas station. He entered into a written contract with Bolly on January 15 in which Bolly agreed to construct a gas station according to specifications incorporated into the writing, in exchange for $250,000. The agreement provided that a progress payment of $100,000 would be made when construction was half complete, and the remainder of the contract price would be paid upon completion. The terms of the writing also specified that work was to begin on March 15 and was to be completed no later than September 15 of the same year, "because Ostek has irrevocably committed to begin purchases of petroleum products on October 1."

On March 1, Bolly telephoned Ostek and stated that due to unanticipated delays in another project, he could not begin construction of the gas station until June 1, and could complete construction no earlier than December 1. When informed that the two-and-a-half month completion delay would result in unacceptable money losses to Ostek, Bolly said, "You've got to give me until December 1 or I can't do the job."

Without further communication with Bolly, on March 10 Ostek entered into a contract with Cantur to construct a gas station on Ostek's land under the same terms as the Ostek-Bolly contract, except that work was to begin April 1, and the total contract price was $300,000. On March 20, Bolly appeared at Ostek's lot and offered to begin construction of the gas station with completion to be by September 15, but Ostek refused to allow him to proceed. On April 1, Cantur commenced construction and subsequently completed the gas station on September 10.

31. What damages should Ostek recover in a breach of contract action against Bolly?

    (A) $50,000, the cost of completion minus the contract price.
    (B) The market value of the gas station as completed minus the contract price.
    (C) The market value of the gas station as completed minus the contract price, plus any incidental damages resulting from the delay in completion.
    (D) $300,000, the cost of completion.

Question 32 refers to the following fact pattern.

Penelope agreed to restore two matching French country farinières (flour boxes). Dennis agreed to pay Penelope $400; however, the agreement did not provide for the time of payment. During Penelope's work on the farinières, Dennis decided to assist Penelope in order to learn more about restoration of antiques. Although Penelope repeatedly protested, Dennis persisted. Dennis damaged several of Penelope's woodworking tools in the process.

32. Assume that Penelope restored one of the farinières and then refused to restore the second one. Dennis hired Regina to complete the job, and pays her $150. If a court finds Penelope's refusal, although in good faith, was not justified, Penelope is entitled to:

    (A) Nothing, because her breach was willful.
    (B) The reasonable value of her services.
    (C) $200, because her original contract was divisible.
    (D) $250, as the difference between the contract price and the cost of completion.

Question 33 refers to the following fact pattern.

Selena holds a profit to mine diamonds on Diamondacre. For many years, she has mined diamonds on a daily basis. Zirconia, who owns Diamondacre, suddenly realizes that he is losing a lot of money by allowing Selena to come onto his property and take the diamonds.

Zirconia plants a six-foot high thorny hedge around Diamondacre so that Selena cannot enter the property. Selena tries to enter by crawling through the hedge but finds it impossible to do so without incurring serious injury.

33. Selena brings an action against Zirconia to require him to remove the hedge and allow her to continue to remove diamonds from Diamondacre. The court will:

    (A) issue a mandatory injunction requiring Zirconia to remove the hedge.
    (B) issue a prohibitory injunction prohibiting Selena from entering the property.
    (C) Both of the above.
    (D) Neither of the above.

Questions 34 and 35 refer to the following fact pattern.

Theresa Tenant has been living in a rented home at 200 Oak Street for about three years. During that time, she has planted a lovely perennial garden where there once was a garbage heap, installed a garbage disposal to correct a chronically clogged drain, and hung a permanent crystal chandelier to lighten up the terminally dark interior of the home.

Oscar Owner discovers that Theresa has altered the property in these ways and becomes incensed. Oscar likes things to look disgusting and does not appreciate the changes Theresa has wrought. He brings an action for injunction and asks the court to require her to return the property to its original condition.

34. How will the court rule?

    (A) For Oscar, as he is the property owner and is entitled to dictate the condition of the property.
    (B) For Oscar, as an injunction is an appropriate remedy here.
    (C) For Theresa, if the changes increase the property value.
    (D) For Theresa, because the house looks better.

35. Assume for the purposes of this question only that Oscar's action is for money damages. What will he recover?

    (A) The cost of removing the alterations Theresa has made.
    (B) The cost of removing the alterations Theresa has made plus the costs of returning the property to its original condition.
    (C) The cost of removing the alterations Theresa has made plus punitive damages, to be determined by the jury.
    (D) Nothing.

ANSWERS TO MULTIPLE CHOICE QUESTIONS

1. (C)

True contracts are those in which the parties' obligation(s) arise from actual agreement and intent. If the agreement or mutual assent is manifested in words (oral or written), the contract is said to be "express." On the other hand, where the mutual undertaking of the parties is *inferred from their conduct* alone, without spoken or written words, the contract is said to be *"implied in fact."* In this hypo, Deke was present while Desmond received the golf lessons from Snead. Even though the parties did not expressly enter into an agreement with respect to Desmond, it is clear from their conduct that an "implied in fact" contract was created. Note that choice (D) is wrong because it addresses quasi-contractual relief. In a quasi-contract, *the parties do not have a contract and the court constructs one to avoid unjust enrichment.* Here, the parties have entered into a contract by their conduct.

2. (D)

Choice (D) is correct because *specific performance is available to enforce a contract for the sale of a unique item of personal property.* Here, the subject matter of the contract (the Ralphio recording) was the only known recording of its kind. As such, Crooner would be entitled to specific performance of the contract. The condition of certification by Prof. Erickson was excused by Collette's conduct when she falsely told Prof. Erickson that the recording was a fake and thus the failure of the condition to occur would not preclude enforcement of the contract.

3. (D)

It is generally accepted that mutual mistake as to the existence of the subject matter is ground for avoidance of a contract. The difficulty lies in determining what is the subject matter. It may be an object, as where A finds a pretty stone and sells it to B for one dollar, and unknown to both A and B it later turns out to an uncut diamond worth one thousand dollars. A may not rescind and recover the stone. The only mistake was as to the value of the object, not as to its existence. On the other hand, not the object, but its rare quality, may be the subject matter, as where A sells to B a stone for two thousand dollars, both of them thinking it to be a diamond, and it turns out to be a zircon, worth about five dollars. B may rescind and recover the price paid, on the ground of mutual mistake as to the existence of the violin as an "original Stradivarius." Therefore, the contract is voidable by Player.

4. (C)

Ordinarily the death of the offeror terminates the power of acceptance created by a revocable offer. But the situation is different when the death occurs after the formation of the contract. Death does not necessarily discharge a contract. If a contract, however, calls for *personal performance by the promisor and person who is to render the performance dies or becomes ill as to make performance impossible,* the *promisor's duty is excused* unless the risk was assumed. Conversely, we have a situation where the promisee, not the promisor, has died. The *doctrine of frustration of purpose* usually applies in these cases. Moreover, where a contract has been discharged for impossibility or frustration, it is often necessary, in the interest of justice, to adjust the rights of the parties. In this situation, recovery for part performance should be available. As a result, choice (C) is correct and Cheri will be entitled to recover the reasonable value of services rendered despite the fact that the contract was discharged by frustration.

5. (A)

This is a "tricky" Contracts question dealing with an interplay between the Statute of Frauds and the "perfect tender" rule. First and foremost, the contract between Maxwell and Scarface is unenforceable under the Statute of Frauds. *The statute requires a contract for the sale of goods of $500 or more to be in writing.* Here, we have an oral contract for the sale of goods totaling $6,000. Therefore, choice (A) is correct. Keep in mind that UCC Section 2-201 provides that the statute does not apply to goods which have been delivered and accepted or for which payment has been made and accepted. In this hypo, Maxwell refused the goods and no payment was made. Many students will incorrectly pick choice (B) and be distracted by the "perfect tender" rule into believing that a breach has occurred. However, the Statute of Frauds renders the oral agreement unenforceable. Therefore, no breach has occurred.

6. (B)

It is important to note that *the doctrine of anticipatory repudiation does not apply in unilateral contracts and in bilateral contracts fully performed on one side.* Where there is an anticipatory repudiation, the injured party may bring an immediate action for total breach. If the doctrine thus applied, choice (C) would have been correct. In this hypo, however, Breeder has fully performed; therefore the doctrine does not apply. As a result, Breeder is only entitled to recover for the partial payment of $250.

7. (A)

When the seller does not deliver (or the buyer properly rejects or revokes acceptance), the buyer's basic remedy is measured by the *difference between the contract price and either the market price or the cover price.* Market price, in measuring the buyer's damages, is determined at the time the buyer learns of the breach under UCC § 2-713. On the other hand, the buyer's remedy of cover, under UCC § 2-712, must be done in good faith and without unreasonable delay. In this question, the cover price was $10 less than the contract price. Gelson's has not lost any money on the purchase, but rather saved $10. Therefore, applying general principles of good faith and mitigation, the buyer is entitled to recover nothing. Choice (A) is correct. Note that an aggrieved buyer is also entitled to any incidental or consequential loss suffered, even though that does not appear to be the case under these facts.

8. (C)

It is universally agreed that the employer may not force an employee to work by means of specific performance. The rationale behind this rule is twofold: (1) money damages are generally available, and (2) it is impossible for courts to properly supervise employment contracts. Here, the question states that this is a suit for specific performance. Thus, choice (C) is the best answer. Note that choice (B) is a good answer but (C) is preferred because it states the proper remedy is at law for money damages.

9. (C)

Many students "shy away" from answer choice (C) under the mistaken belief that a plaintiff was required to make an election of remedies choice between money damages or injunctive relief. Restatement of Torts 2d, Section 951, states, however, that "*in an action for injunction the court may, in addition to or in lieu of injunction, give one or more of the following remedies: (1) a judgment for damages; (2) a judgment for the recovery of possession of land or chattels, or (3) a declaratory judgment.*" In order to avoid unnecessary litigation, courts having equity powers commonly award damages for torts committed prior to or pending suit, in addition to an injunction, in the same action. Choice (C) is thus the best answer because Biggerstaff's property value has diminished 20% due to the operation of the slaughterhouse. Consequently, damages would be an appropriate remedy to compensate the plaintiff for his financial loss. In addition, the court should also grant injunctive relief to prevent the nuisance from continuing in this residential neighborhood.

10. (C)

This is a "tricky" contracts question dealing with damages. Many students will be tempted to choose choice (D) because the facts state that Neptune assumed the risk that it might not receive government approval for the satellite system. However, choice (D) is incorrect because the facts also indicate that Solar Systems would be paid the $3,000,000 contract price *upon completion of the satellite*. Clearly, Neptune is repudiating the contract before completion. Under the circumstances, Solar Systems would normally be entitled to the contract cost less the amount it would have cost to complete the job. However, the facts state that the cost of completion cannot be calculated. As a consequence, that answer choice would not be correct. (C) is the best answer choice because it recognizes that sellers are entitled to incidental damages in addition to their general damages. See UCC § 2-703.

REMEDIES FOR BREACH OF CONTRACT

A. The interests of the aggrieved party. Whenever a party suffers a material breach of contract, at least three interests are immediately threatened.

   1. The restitution interest: If on the date of the breach the aggrieved party has already wholly or partially performed his own contract obligations, a material breach on the part of the other trader leaves the breaching party unjustly enriched by the value of that performance, and the aggrieved party unjustly impoverished by its cost.

   2. The reliance test: If on the date of the breach the aggrieved party has not yet performed his own contract obligations, but has incurred expenses or forgone other opportunities in reliance upon the expectation that the other would

perform, the breaching party is not unjustly enriched, but the out of pocket loss to the aggrieved party represents unjust impoverishment.

3. The expectation interest: If, on the date of the breach, the aggrieved party has neither performed his own contract obligations nor changed position in detrimental reliance on the promise of the breaching party to perform, there is neither unjust present enrichment of the breaching party nor unjust present impoverishment of the aggrieved party. There is, however, a disappointment of expectations of future wealth or future advantage that would have been gained had the breaching party performed.

11. (A)

Here, students must recognize that Alarmco is obligated under the terms of its contract with Ohner to install the security system for $12,000. The mere fact that Supplier refused to perform would not excuse Alarmco from its duties under the agreement with Ohner. By agreeing to perform the installation work, Alarmco assumed the risks attendant with producing that result.

12. (A)

According to UCC § 2-713, the measure of damages for non-delivery or repudiation by the seller is the difference between the market price at the time when the buyer learned of the breach and the contract price together with any incidental and consequential damages as provided under Section 2-715. Note that recovery for the contract price is inappropriate because the buyer's proper remedy is either to "cover" or seek damages measured by Section 2-713. Since damages at law are adequate, specific performance will not be decreed.

13. (B)

In accordance with UCC § 2-706, a seller may resell goods after the buyer has repudiated or breached the contract. Where the resale is made in good faith and in a commercially reasonable manner the seller may recover the difference between the resale price and the contract price together with incidental damages. Since McCormick resold the goods to Western for $50,000 (or the same amount as National promised to pay), McCormick can recover only incidental damages.

14. (B)

Vito was in breach of contract by refusing to accept Medford's milk delivery. Consequently, Medford's measure of damages would be the resale loss (i.e., the difference between the contract price and the resale). Note that cover is a remedy for buyers, not sellers, thus A is incorrect. Revocation of acceptance is a remedy of a buyer for a non-conforming goods and does not apply to offers so D is incorrect.

15. (B)

The July 16, 2008, agreement between Arthur and Dexter created a legally enforceable contract. Therefore, Dexter's unjustified failure to perform (i.e., his refusal to lend Arthur the $50,000) when performance was due constituted a breach of contract, which entitled the injured party to damages. Alternative (A) is incorrect because *anticipatory repudiation occurs if one party to an executory bilateral contract repudiates the contract in advance of the time set for performance by announcing that he will not perform it.* In the present case, Dexter did not repudiate in advance but rather he did not render his performance when it was due (or upon Arthur's request for the loan).

16. (C)

Be aware that choices (A) and (B) are incorrect because *quantum meruit* (i.e, reasonable value for services rendered) is a restitutionary form of relief. In this particular situation, the plaintiff's proper form of relief is damages for breach of contract, not restitution. Where plaintiff has fully performed his side of the contract, and the defendant's only duty is the payment of the agreed price in money, the remedy of restitution of the value of his performance is *not* available to the plaintiff. His proper remedy is damages for breach. See Restatement 2d of Contracts section 373(2).

17. (C)

This is a rather tricky question. It is important to point out that Sprink was hired to perform the replacement work at a contract price of $2,400. According to the terms of the agreement, Sprink would be paid *upon completion of the job*. As such, the contract does not appear to be divisible. Therefore, choice (A) is wrong. Although Sprink did not complete performance, he would, nevertheless, be entitled to receive restitution for the part performance that he rendered. A recovery on *quantum meruit* usually applies in situations where the plaintiff has performed services for the defendant but he cannot recover on the contract (either because there was not full performance or because the contract was unenforceable).

18. (A)

The basic damages goal, where the landowner breaches a construction contract, is to give the building contractor his expectancy. Where he has fully performed his contract by delivering the structure contracted for, he is entitled to recover the full contract price, just as in any other case where full performance creates a liquidated debt. At the other end of the spectrum, the landowner may repudiate the contract before the contractor has done any work or bought any materials at all. In such a case the policy of giving the contractor his expectancy is carried out by giving him the profit he would have made on the contract, and this is normally done by giving him the contract price minus the cost of complying with the contract. The more common and more difficult situation occurs where the contractor has done a portion of the work under the contract before the owner breaches. In that situation the basic rule is the contractor is entitled to recover *the contract price, less the savings he effects because he is not required to complete the job.*

19. (A)

Assuming that Contractor is liable, what damages (for breach of contract) may Ohner recover? The rule as to the measure of damages is that the plaintiff is, so far as money can do it, to be placed in the same situation as if the contract had been performed. As such, choice (A) is correct because Ohner will be entitled to $2,000 or the *loss of bargain measure of money damages.* In the absence of special circumstances, the loss of bargain is measured as the difference, if any, between the contract price and the reasonable cost of the substitute performance. The only benefit of his bargain compensable at law is the difference, if any, between what he had promised to pay for that performance in the future and the cost of that performance from another source on the day it should have been furnished. Since Ohner was only obligated to pay $22,000, his recovery should be limited to $2,000, the difference between Contractor's price and Carpenter's price.

20. (D)

As a general rule, damages for breach by either party may be liquidated in the agreement but only at an amount that is reasonable in the light of the anticipated or actual loss caused by the breach and the difficulties of proof of loss. However, *a term fixing unreasonably large liquidated damages is unenforceable on grounds of public policy as a penalty.* Note that a determination whether the amount fixed is a penalty turns on the following two factors: (1) whether the amount fixed is reasonable to the extent that it approximates the loss anticipated at the time of the making of the contract and (2) difficulty of proof of loss. If the difficulty of proof of loss is great, considerable latitude is allowed in the approximation of anticipated or actual harm. Where, however, it is clear that *no loss at all has occurred, a majority of courts find a provision fixing a substantial sum as damages is unenforceable.* Since the Kent Highway Department failed to complete its half of the bridge, Valvano's delay did not cause Concord Highway Department any loss. Choice (D) is therefore correct.

21. (B)

Note that choice (A) is wrong because the Statute of Frauds is inapplicable. *The Statute of Frauds requires that contracts for the sale of goods of over $500 must be in writing.* The agreement between Irving and Joel does not cover the sale of goods. Choice (B) is the best answer because nominal damages are recoverable for breach where the plaintiff has suffered no pecuniary injury or where the loss is too speculative to be provided with certainty. The reason why (B) is correct and not (C) is because Irving suffered no pecuniary injury. It is necessary to remember that Irving's debt to Harry was barred by the statute of limitations. Consequently, Irving was not legally obligated to pay Harry anything. As a result, Irving did not suffer any pecuniary loss for Joel's failure to perform, other than the loss of his T-shirt. In the absence of proof of the value of the shirt, Irving is limited to nominal damages. Choice (D) is likewise wrong because specific performance is only available *if the remedy at law is inadequate*. The legal remedy is adequate (i.e., nominal damages).

22. (B)

Since the encroachment of the fence violated the restriction (i.e., equitable servitude), Wilber would be entitled to injunctive relief. Choice (A) is incorrect since the restriction would be construed as an equitable servitude, rather than an easement. Choices (C) and (D) are incorrect because any lot owner in Del Mar may enforce the restriction.

23. (C)

Traditionally, one party's unilateral mistake as to an element of the contract would justify rescission only if the other party knew or reasonably should have known of the mistake and took advantage of the mistaken party's error. Choice (C) identifies this principle in the context of the question. Because George was unaware of and had no reason to know of Peter's accounting error, such a unilateral mistake does not authorize Peter to rescind the contract that was formed when George accepted his sub-bid. (A modern approach to unilateral mistakes permits the mistaken party to rescind if (a) the mistake goes to a basic assumption of the contract and (b) the hardship to the mistaken party from enforcement of the contract substantially outweighs the detriment to the non-mistaken party caused by rescission so that enforcement of the contract would be unconscionable. There is nothing in the facts to indicate that the hardship of the $50,000 mistake would be any less detrimental to George than to Peter.) (A) is incorrect. The fact that Peter's error costs him the benefit of his bargain, which probably means his profit, is not alone enough to justify rescission based on his unilateral mistake. The principles discussed above in connection with choice (C) determine when rescission is available for unilateral mistake. Since George did not know or have reason to know of Peter's error, and since the conditions for rescission even under the modern approach are not present, Peter may not rescind. (B) is inaccurate. A unilateral mistake of the kind made by Peter does not rob the parties of mutual assent, because both agreed to what they thought were the terms of the contract, and neither was mistaken as to what those terms were. The mistake of one party as to the basis for his proposed contract terms has no effect on the mutual assent as to those terms. (D) is not the best choice. As indicated above, a unilateral mistake can be the basis for rescission by the mistaken party if the non-mistaken party knows or should have known of the mistake and takes advantage of it, or if the more modern conditions for rescission are present. Thus, choice (D) goes too far and is an inaccurate statement of law. Since it reaches the right result on faulty reasoning, choice (D) is not the best answer.

24. (B)

The tremendous disparity between Peter's sub-bid in this question—$360,000—and the competing sub-bids, which the facts state were at least $10,000 higher than the $510,000 sub-bid originally described, should have alerted George to the fact that there was an error in the sub-bid, and his acceptance in effect took knowing advantage of Peter's unilateral error. Where the non-mistaken party knows or should have known of the mistaken party's unilateral error, and takes advantage of it, the mistaken party is entitled to rescind. (A) is not the best choice. The non-mistaken party is not required to investigate all bids or even to investigate any bid, unless some fact comes to light that would alert a reasonable person to a mistake by the other party. Here the great difference between Peter's sub-bid as transmitted and the competing plumbing sub-bids would have caused a reasonable person to investigate, which would have revealed the telegraph company error. Choice (A) is wrong because it places too great a burden on the nonmistaken party. (C) is incorrect. George has no contractual relationship with the telegraph company, and thus no basis for any remedy as to that party. Additionally, George's rights against a third party do not affect the right to rescind where George knew or should have known of the error. Neither is George responsible for an error introduced by the company. Peter is the only one with a claim against the telegraph company, and must bear responsibility for the telegraph error. (D) is inaccurate. An adhesion contract is one where the disparate position and bargaining powers of the two parties means that one, the weaker, must take the agreement as dictated by the stronger, or have no agreement at all. Contracts between commercial parties are rarely, if ever, adhesion contracts because each has a relatively equal position to negotiate from.

25. (C)

UCC §2-716(1) authorizes specific performance in favor of the buyer where the goods are unique or in "other proper circumstances." A puppy is certainly unique in the same respects that make individual humans unique, if not viewed entirely as a commodity. The circumstances of the contract, Lady apparently being a dog of unequalled perfection, establish that an alternative mother might not provide a fungible set of qualities. In addition, all of the other answers are patently wrong. (A) is incorrect. By any measure of damages, Clavin would not be entitled to recover the contract price. The standard measure of damages where the seller breaches is the difference between the market price at the time of breach and the contract price, plus incidental and consequential damages, and less expenses saved. The facts state that comparable pups sell for, at most, $2,500, so by measure of damages Clavin has not suffered any damages at all. ($2,500 minus $3,000 equals no damages.) All the more reason to grant specific performance. (B) is inaccurate. Choice (B) purposefully reverses the proper measure of damages, which is market price ($2,500) minus contract price ($3,000), in order to confuse and obfuscate. In fact, Clavin can show no money damages from Himtodt's breach. (D) is incorrect. Because, as discussed above, there are no money damages to be had, let alone $3,000, the contract price, choice (D) must be in error in including them as viable options of Clavin.

26. (C)

A buyer who rejects nonconforming goods is entitled to recover any prepayment; he can also resell any nonconforming accepted goods under his duty to mitigate damages and then apply the proceeds to the amount owed to him by the seller for the nonconformity. Here, Beau paid Samuel $2,500 on receipt of the 250 pounds of Agee, but later rejected 200 pounds; as a result, Samuel would be expected to refund $2,000. Since

Beau impliedly accepted 50 pounds of the chemical by placing it in production, Beau is due no refund from Samuel on that 50 pounds. (A) is wrong. Since Beau properly rejected 200 pounds of the chemical as nonconforming, Beau can recover his prepayment for those pounds, as explained above. (B) is incorrect. There is no reason why Beau cannot recover all of the $2,000 prepaid for the chemical he ultimately rejected as nonconforming. (D) is wrong. Beau can resell the chemicals he has accepted and then apply the proceeds to the amount of damages owed to him by Samuel as a result of the nonconformity.

27. (B)

Under UCC §2-715, an aggrieved buyer may recover *incidental damages* resulting from a seller's breach. These incidental damages include expenses reasonably incurred in inspection, receipt, transportation, and care and custody of goods rightfully rejected. Since the goods delivered were nonconforming and, therefore, rightfully rejected, Beau can recover the inspection and storage costs of the Agee as incidental damages. (A) is wrong. Punitive damages are not available in breach of contract actions. Beau would need to add a tort cause of action to his breach of contract suit in order to recover punitive damages, and the facts do not support any tort actions of the nature that would allow such damages to be awarded (e.g., intentional conduct). (C) is not the best choice. *Consequential damages* may be recovered only if reasonably *foreseeable* by a person in the breaching party's position at the formation of the contract and if they can be proven with reasonable *certainty*. Here, damages for delay in placing the new cheese on the market would probably be too speculative to recover. Under the facts, the Food and Drug Administration test results had not even been released yet, and there are no facts stated to indicate that Beau could prove with certainty that he suffered any losses due to the delay in placing the cheese on the market. (B) is a better choice because incidental damages are clearly recoverable by an aggrieved buyer. (D) is incorrect. In order to receive damages for mental suffering, Beau must add a tort action to his breach of contract suit. As indicated above, the facts do not support such a recovery.

28. (C)

The standard measure of damages recoverable by a seller of goods is the difference between the unpaid contract price and the market price at the time and place of tender, plus incidental expenses and less any expenses saved as the result of the breach. (UCC §2-708(1).) However, where the standard measure is inadequate to put the seller in as good a position as performance, as where the breach results in lost volume that is not replaced by resale, the measure of damages is lost profits including reasonable overhead plus incidental damages and cost incurred. (UCC §2-708(2).) Here, the Electron Store can obtain as many Walk-'n-Talkmans as it sells, and the resale of Bueller's Walk-'n-Talkman to Calistoga represented an already existing sale that would have occurred independently of Bueller's breach. That is, Electron Store lost one sale and the profit from that sale by Bueller's breach. The seller is entitled to the profit it would have earned from both the sale to Bueller and sale of another Walk-'n-Talkman to Calistoga. The Electron Store's profit is $1,000 ($2,500 retail price minus $1,500 cost from the factory), of which $300 must be offset for Bueller's down payment. Although the UCC permits a court to refuse to enforce an unconscionable contract, there are no facts here to suggest oppressive terms or sales tactics. The mere use of a standard form does not justify a finding of unconscionability. (B) reflects the typical contract measure of damages, which are inadequate in a lost volume sale situation such as this. (D) is inaccurate. Choice (D) gives the seller too much, because it awards the entire contract price without considering the cost that the Electron Store had to pay to the manufacturer for each Walk-'n-Talkman that it sold. The seller is entitled to lost *profit*, which is retail price minus cost to the seller.

29. (A)

In a construction contract where the builder breaches, the owner's standard measure of expectation damages is the cost of completion. However, where the builder's breach is the result of deficient performance by a subcontractor and the cost to complete would be disproportionate to the benefit received by the owner, the owner may be entitled to recover as damages the diminution of value of the construction as built compared to how it should have been built. Here, then, Developer must pay Contractor the contract price for the work substantially performed, minus the diminished value of the restaurant caused by the defective wall covering. (B) is wrong. The measure of damages in this instance of deficient performance is contract price less diminution in value, not the full contract price. Even where a contract has been substantially performed, the aggrieved party can recover damages for the minor breach. (C) is not the best choice. Though it is true that, in a proper delegation, obligee Developer would have a direct action for breach of contract against the delegates, Sub, he would retain all of his rights against the obligor, Contractor, since there was no novation. Also, the measure of damages in this situation is contract price minus diminution in value, not the full contract price. (D) is incorrect. Where a party has not performed exactly as promised but has completed a substantial portion of the performance due, although technically in breach, the substantial performance will mature the other party's obligation, and the injured party will be entitled to an offset for damages. Here, though the wall covering did not match exactly, "it was otherwise functional," thereby meeting the standard for substantial performance.

30. (C)

Contract damages should give the aggrieved party what he expected from the bargain and, to the extent that money can do so, the aggrieved party should be placed in the same position as if the contract had been fully performed. Where the employee breaches an employment contract, the standard measure of damages equals any additional compensation paid for a substitute employee. Here, Firm expended $500 extra for the substitute in each January and February and would expend an additional $500 per month over the amount for which Lawyer had agreed to work. Therefore, Firm may recover $ 1,000 in damages for the first two months (since that money has already been paid), as well as the discounted present value of $500 for the months March through December (since that money has not already been paid). (A) is incorrect. Damages of $500 will not give Firm its expectation from the bargain, since it expected to have that position filled for $48,000 per year. (B) is wrong. Since Firm expected to have the work performed by Lawyer for $48,000 year and instead will pay an extra $500 per month to have the same work performed by Associate, Firm is entitled to recover all damages resulting from Lawyer's breach. (D) is wrong. An aggrieved party need not investigate the reason for the breach in order to be entitled to recover for the breach.

31. (A)

The standard measure of damages recoverable by an aggrieved owner where the builder breaches a construction contract is the cost of completion to the owner compared to the price of the breached contract, which in this problem would be $50,000. (B) and (C) are incorrect. Using the market value of the completed gas station as the measure of damages would not put the owner in the same position as if the original contract had not been breached. Compensating the owner for the increase cost of construction does, as (A) indicates. (D) is wrong. Awarding the owner the entire cost of completion would place him in a much better position than would have performance by the wrongdoer. Some consideration must be given to what the owner originally expected to pay for the completed building. Ostek's damages are the additional amount he had to pay to build the gas station on time.

32. (B)

A breaching party's remedy is limited to restitution as measured by the reasonable value of the services provided. Some courts may limit this to instances of breaches that are not willful, however, Penelope's breach was unjustified but not in bad faith. Courts will permit her to recover the reasonable value of her services, making (B) correct. A breaching party may not recover on the contract unless the court finds the contract divisible. This contract was not for two farinieres at $200 per fariniere, but $400 for the services to be provided and is therefore not divisible, making (C) incorrect. (D) is incorrect because the difference between the contract price and the cost to complete is the measure of recovery for one paying for the service, not the one providing the service.

33. (A)

Incorporeal interests in land are considered to be unique and injunctions are therefore appropriate. A mandatory injunction requiring Zirconia to remove the hedge is the most likely result of the litigation. (B) is incorrect because Selena has done nothing to deprive herself of the right to enter, the court will allow Selena to continue collecting diamonds. (C) and (D) are therefore incorrect answers.

34. (C)

Where a tenant improves the land in such a way that the property value is increased, equitable relief will not be granted because it is not possible to show irreparable injury. (B) is therefore incorrect. (A) is incorrect because the court will not require Theresa to reverse improvements that increase the property's value. (D), while not a bad answer, does not address the requirement that the property value increase.

35. (D)

Oscar's property has increased in value. Therefore, he is not entitled to money damages — there is no diminution in the value of the property.

Note to students: Because Remedies is an interdisciplinary subject, you may encounter essay questions that require you to draw on your knowledge of contract, tort, property, and constitutional law. The same will undoubtedly be true on your law school exams and on the bar exam!

Questions 1 and 2 refer to the following fact pattern.

Al planned to build a large shopping center in a suburban area. Betty agreed in writing to sell Al her 100-acre farm located in the center of the proposed development. Al deposited with Betty a portion of the purchase price, the balance to be paid upon delivery of the deed by Betty. At the time their written contract was entered into, Al told Betty only that he was buying her land and 200 acres from other local farmers for a "big project."

Relying upon Betty's agreement, Al purchased the surrounding 200 acres from other farmers. He paid them the same price he had contracted to pay Betty: $1,000 an acre. This price was $200 an acre over market value.

Claude, hoping to build his own shopping center on other nearby land, paid Betty $100,000 to refuse to convey her property to Al. Betty falsely notified Al that she could not complete the sale because she had discovered a defect in her title. Al reluctantly accepted return of his deposit. Without Betty's land, Al could not develop the shopping center as planned, and he has offered his 200 acres for sale. Claude's shopping center is nearing completion.

Al recently learned of Claude's arrangements with Betty.

What legal and equitable remedies does Al have:

1. Against Betty? Discuss.
2. Against Claude? Discuss.

Questions 3–5 refer to the following fact pattern.

Alice took her diamond ring worth $14,000 to Bob, a jeweler, to have the stone reset. After Bob had agreed to reset the stone and Alice had left the shop, Bob placed the ring on a counter for a few minutes while he helped another customer. Carl, also a customer, took Alice's ring and left the shop.

Carl later sold the ring for $15,000. He deposited $2,000 of the proceeds in a savings account that already contained $5,000 of his own funds, and bought Blackacre with the remaining $13,000.

When Alice returned for her ring, Bob told her that it had been stolen, that he thought he knew the identity of the thief, that he had hired a private investigator, and that he hoped to recover the ring. The investigator's activities prompted Carl to admit his theft.

Blackacre is now worth $26,000. The balance in Carl's savings account, which had dropped to a low of $600 after he had deposited the $2,000, is now $3,000.

Carl has revealed that he sold the ring to Dan, who knew nothing about Carl's theft.

3. What are Alice's rights and to what relief against Bob, if any, is she entitled? Discuss.

4. What are Alice's rights and to what relief against Carl, if any, is she entitled? Discuss.

5. What are Alice's rights and to what relief against Dan, if any, is she entitled? Discuss.

Questions 6 and 7 refer to the following fact pattern.

Al owns Blackacre, a country property with extensive highway frontage. Blackacre adjoins property on which the Restview Inn is located. Two years ago, after prolonged discussion, Al said to his son-in-law, Bret, "I grant you the right to construct and maintain 10 billboards on Blackacre to advertise your business." No consideration was agreed to or paid. The statement was overhead by Carl, an attorney and mutual friend. Al and Bret previously had asked Carl what words they should use to put their intentions into effect.

Immediately thereafter, Bret erected 10 large, neon-lighted billboards. Each cost in excess of $2,500. The billboards dominate the landscape as seen from the adjacent Restview Inn, which for more than 25 years prior to the erection of the billboards had been very popular with vacationers desiring to escape the urban sprawl and to enjoy the unobstructed view of the natural countryside. One billboard blocks the view and cuts off the sunlight to one side of the Inn's dining room.

Peter, the owner of Restview Inn, is threatening to sue Al if he does not remove the billboards, and Bret is threatening to sue Al if he does.

6. What are the rights and remedies, if any, of Peter against Al? Discuss.

7. What are the rights and remedies, if any, of Bret against Al? Discuss.

Question 8 refers to the following fact pattern.

Sam owned Blackacre and Whiteacre, two unimproved vacant tracts of land. The county assessor's records listed each tract as containing ten acres. Without having seen either tract, but having checked the assessor's records, Bob telephoned Sam and said, "I offer to buy Blackacre and Whiteacre for $20,000—$10,000 now and $10,000 in one year." Sam responded, "O.K., I'll have the papers ready tomorrow." The following day Bob paid Sam $10,000, and the parties signed a land sale contract prepared by Sam's lawyer. The contract described the property as "Blackacre, containing 20 acres, more or less," and did not mention Whiteacre. The contract was otherwise consistent with the oral communications between Bob and Sam.

The contract did not contain language making time of the essence.

During the next 12 months the following events occurred:

A. Bob sold his interest in the contract to Cal for $10,000. Cal notified Sam of his purchase.
B. The announcement of a proposed freeway increased land values in the area from $1,000 per acre to $3,000 per acre.

C. Bob, Sam, and Cal each learned that, while Blackacre contained ten acres, Whiteacre contained only seven acres.

On the date the final payment was due, Cal tendered $7,000 to Sam and demanded deeds to Blackacre and Whiteacre. Sam rejected the tender and two days later notified Cal that the purchaser's interest in the contract was "terminated because of non-payment."

Land values in the area are continuing to increase rapidly.

8. What rights and remedies, if any, does Cal have? Discuss.

Question 9 refers to the following fact pattern.

Corp, Inc. (Corp) has 200,000 authorized shares of $1 par value stock. Andy, Ben, Carl, and Dave each purchased at par and continue to hold 50,000 shares of Corp. Corp's articles prohibit incurring any single debt in excess of $75,000 and require a vote representing 80 percent of outstanding shares to amend the articles. The articles also provided for preemptive rights, cumulative voting, and a board of four directors. Each of the four shareholders has elected himself director at annual shareholder meetings during each year of corporate existence.

Corp's board unanimously decided to borrow $100,000 from Lender. Lender took Corp's ten-year note, bearing interest at 20 percent per annum, payable in monthly interest installments. Corp has the option to pay off the note at any time, without penalty. Later, Lender needed funds and approached Andy, who serves as Corp's treasurer. Lender offered to sell the note for $90,000 and Andy, without consulting with Ben, Carl, or Dave, purchased the note on his own account.

The week following the purchase of the note by Andy, Rich asked to subscribe to 100,000 shares of Corp stock at $1 per share. Ben, Carl, and Dave approved Rich's proposal, but at the annual shareholders' meeting, Andy voted against and thus defeated a proposed amendment of the articles authorizing additional shares free from preemptive rights. Because of the note's high interest, Andy did not want it paid off. The other directors, hoping to use Rich's investment to pay the note and now aware of Andy's acquisition of it, were angered and caused Corp to cease paying the monthly interest installments.

Rich then caused the incorporation of Endrun, Inc., and subscribed to 100,000 of its shares for $100,000. Rich proposes that Corp be merged into Endrun, that each Corp share be converted into an Endrun share, and that Endrun pay the Lender note now held by Andy. Corp's board has approved the merger three to one, Andy dissenting.

Assume that the interest rate is not usurious.

9. Can Andy obtain an injunction to prevent the Corp-Endrun merger? Discuss.

Question 10 refers to the following fact pattern.

Owen owned an unzoned 50-acre tract that was unimproved. He divided it into 45 one-acre lots with access roads. Owen offered the 45 lots for sale and told each prospective purchaser of the purely residential nature of the entire 50-acre tract. He sold 30 of the lots to 30 different purchasers and retained ownership of a block of 15 contiguous lots located on the easterly edge of the tract. The deed delivered to each purchaser contains the following language:

> "The grantee agrees for himself and his successors in title that the land hereby

conveyed shall be used only for residential purposes and no structure other than a single-family residence together with appropriate out-buildings shall be constructed thereon."

Within five years of the first of Owen's sales, all of the 30 purchasers had recorded their deeds from Owen and had built substantial one-family residences on their lots.

Within 15 years of the first of Owen's sales, land surrounding the 50-acre tract was substantially developed and became of a mixed residential and commercial character. This development resulted in a great increase in the value of Owen's 15 remaining lots for commercial use. Owen then sold those remaining lots to Bob, who has now commenced construction of a shopping center.

Prior to purchasing Owen's lots, Bob asked Owen if there were any restrictions on those lots, and Owen told him there were none. Bob also examined Owen's direct chain of title prior to his purchase and discovered no indications of the restrictions.

The owners of the original 30 lots (Homeowners) learned of the sale by Owen to Bob and Bob's intended use of the 15 lots only when the shopping center construction began. Homeowners promptly objected to Bob about his construction, contending that he is restricted to using the 15 lots he purchased from Owen for single-family residence purposes. They also contend that the shopping center will generate excessive traffic, exhaust fumes, and noise near their homes.

10. What are Homeowners' rights and remedies against Bob? Discuss.

Question 11 refers to the following fact pattern.

Proff agreed to deliver a lecture at State College on January 10, 1985, for which he was to receive a $10,000 fee. On December 31, 1984, he went to Flyright Travel Co. to ask about flights to State College. He told a Flyright employee that he had to be at State College by 3:00 P.M. When told that Midwest Flight #1, which left at noon, would get him to State College by 1:30 P.M., Proff purchased a reserved seat, nonrefundable super discount ticket on that flight. The ticket, prepared by the Flyright employee, bore both the flight number and departure time stated by the Flyright employee.

Proff arrived at the airport at 11:30 A.M. on January 10, ample time to check in and pass through security at that airport, but discovered then that Flight #1 had departed at 11:25 A.M. in conformity with a new schedule that had been sent on December 1, 1984, to all travel agents authorized to sell Midwest tickets. Flyright had received the new schedule on December 5 but had not entered the change in the computer data used by its employees. Because no alternative transportation was available, Proff could not deliver his lecture. In response to a State College demand, he returned a $5,000 advance he had received from the school.

On January 5, 1987, Proff filed an action against Flyright to recover damages. He alleged in his complaint that the damages were incurred because Flyright's negligence made it impossible for him to deliver the lecture and he therefore lost the lecture fee and the cost of the ticket. He also sought punitive damages.

Flyright seeks dismissal of Proff's complaint, by a procedurally proper motion.

11. How should the court rule on the following grounds urged in support of the motion to dismiss? "Even if the complaint states a cause of action, the damages sought cannot be recovered by any theory suggested by the facts alleged." Discuss.

Questions 12–14 refer to the following fact pattern.

Without seeking bids from other contractors, Owen entered into a written contract on March 2, with Cobb, a contractor, whereby Cobb was to remodel Owen's house for $20,000. The remodeling was such that Owen could continue to live in his home while Cobb worked on it.

Owen paid Cobb $2,000 when the contract was signed. The contract called for payment of the $18,000 balance upon completion of the work and for completion by November 1 of the same year. The contract also provides that in the event of delay in completion, the amount due Cobb from Owen would be reduced by $500 for each month, or part thereof, of delay.

When Cobb had completed 50 percent of the work, he informed Owen that he would not finish the remodeling at the contract price. He told Owen that he had underestimated labor costs by $4,000 as a result of a mathematical error made by his bookkeeper. Owen refused to agree to pay a higher amount, and Cobb refused to proceed with the remodeling.

Owen promptly obtained bids from two other contractors for completion of the work. He accepted the lower of the two bids: $15,000. Included in this bid was $1,500 to remove and replace paneling Cobb had installed in the family room. Cobb had installed a much lighter weight paneling than called for by the contract. The substitute contractor completed the remodeling, including replacement of the paneling, on December 1.

Cobb sued Owen to recover the value of work he did up to the time he stopped performance. Owen counterclaimed for damages stemming from Cobb's refusal to fulfill the contract and for $500 based on late completion of the work.

Are the following rulings of the trial judge (who sat without a jury) correct? Discuss.

12. Cobb had breached the contract but could recover $8,000 on his claim;

13. Cobb's recovery would be offset by $5,000, as damages owing to Owen based on Cobb's breach of the contract; and

14. Owen could not recover any amount based on the liquidated damages clause in the contract.

Question 15 refers to the following fact pattern.

Paul recently moved into the area to open a new restaurant. After months of searching for a personal residence, Paul offered to purchase Seller's house. With his new restaurant soon to open, Paul hired Chef to head up his kitchen staff under an agreement that allows either party to terminate the employment relationship on thirty days' notice. Paul entered into a written three-year contract with Meatco, a food supplier, for regular weekly deliveries of high quality meat.

Dan, owner of ten restaurants, learned about all of the above and resolved to do what he could to hinder the operation of Paul's new restaurant. Dan offered Chef double his current salary and told Chef that if he did not quit his job with Paul, "I can make it difficult for you to get your next job. I have many restaurant connections all over the country, you know."

Dan wrote to Meatco: "It has come to my attention that you are supplying Paul. In all candor, I must tell you that so long as you continue to do so, I will not deal with you once our contract ends in two weeks."

Dan then offered Seller a much higher price for his house than that offered by Paul, hoping that recommencing a house search would divert Paul's attention from operating his restaurant.

Chef terminated his employment with Paul and went to work for Dan. Meatco stopped deliveries to Paul. Seller accepted Dan's offer for the house.

Paul's restaurant opened but incurred significant losses. Paul's reputation in the restaurant community was adversely affected. Meanwhile, Dan's restaurants flourished.

Paul sues Dan.

15. What are Paul's rights and remedies, if any, against Dan? Discuss.

Question 16 refers to the following fact pattern.

For seven years, Refin has been operating a smelter within Zone A of City. A major portion of Refin's operations is the crushing of ores, which produces considerable noise and dust. City's zoning ordinance permits a smelter to operate in Zone A. Last year, several residential subdivisions, the nearest a mile from the smelter but all inside Zone A, were developed and occupied.

Residents of the new subdivisions are concerned because Refin trucks haul granular toxic chemicals in covered drums from a supply depot to the smelter on a regular basis. The only reasonable route to the smelter from the depot is over a street that borders the residential subdivisions. Recently, a cover on one of the drums was blown off by a strong wind; chemicals were scattered and, while causing no personal injuries, badly burned the lawns of four homeowners.

Refin's procedures for disposing of chemical residue also concern the residents. Employees bury the residue in containers that, because of internal chemical action, will decompose after 10 to 15 years. Chemically active materials could then invade a nearby lake, the source of the subdivision's main water supply. The residue containers used by Refin are the most durable that are available for sealing the chemical residue.

Residents have urged City to bring suit against Refin, but City has not yet acted. However, Howard, one of those who urged action by City and whose lawn was badly damaged by the chemicals blown by the wind, has sued Refin seeking damages and equitable relief.

16. What are Howard's rights and remedies, if any? Discuss.

Questions 17–20 refer to the following fact pattern.

Henry was an agent for Insco. Over a period of several months, he embezzled a total of $50,000. The shortage in his accounts was not discovered until after Henry died, one month after his final embezzlement.

Henry gave $5,000 of the embezzled money to the Red Cross.

Henry deposited $25,000 of the embezzled money in his savings account at Bank. At the time of the deposit, the account contained $20,000 of Henry's own money. He later withdrew $30,000 from the account, all of which he lost in a week of betting at a race track. Using his own money from his then-current earnings, Henry bought a lottery ticket on which he won $15,000, all of which he deposited in the savings account. That was the last transaction involving the account before Henry died.

Henry spent $10,000 of the embezzled money for the premium on a life insurance policy on which his wife, Susan, is the beneficiary. The policy had a face value of $100,000, and the insurance company paid that amount to Susan upon Henry's death. Susan was not aware of the policy or the embezzlement until after Henry's death. Susan has invested the $100,000 in a certificate of deposit.

Insco is able to determine the foregoing but is unable to determine what Henry did with the remaining $10,000 of the embezzled money. The inventory in Henry's probate estate lists the savings account at Bank and personal property worth $10,000. Insco cannot establish that any of the embezzled funds were used to acquire any of the personal property in the estate.

What are Insco's rights and remedies against:

17. The Red Cross? Discuss.

18. The funds in Henry's savings account with Bank? Discuss.

19. Susan's certificate of deposit? Discuss.

20. The personal property in Henry's estate? Discuss.

Questions 21 and 22 refer to the following fact pattern.

Peter owned a sporting goods store. He learned that American Building Company ("ABC") was about to construct a shopping mall in his city. Desirous of expanding his business, he approached ABC to arrange to rent a small space in the proposed mall. A lease agreement for a small store to be located in the East Wing of the mall was signed by Peter and ABC on July 1, 1991. Although the dimensions of the space and its proposed rent are recited in the agreement, no provision is made for an exact date when the space would be completed and ready for occupancy. The agreement explicitly leaves the determination of when the East Wing of the mall will be built to the judgment of ABC.

On August 1, 1991, Peter learned through a newspaper column that ABC had agreed with a toy company to lease to it the entire East Wing of the mall, including the area where Peter's store would have been located. Feeling that he had a valid contract, Peter took no immediate action; he thought that ABC would eventually accommodate him either by extending existing plans for that part of the mall or by offering him alternative space elsewhere in the mall.

In March 1992, Peter inquired of ABC when he might expect his space to be ready for occupancy. He was informed that ABC had changed its plans and was in the process of building a structure in which it would rent space in the East Wing to four or five major lessees, not including Peter, and that there would be no space elsewhere in the mall for Peter.

In an action by Peter against ABC in state court in State X, Peter has obtained an *ex parte* temporary restraining order halting construction.

21. Is Peter entitled to a preliminary injunction against ABC restraining it from proceeding with construction based on the changed building plans? Discuss.

22. Can Peter eventually force ABC to build and lease to him a space as described in the lease agreement of July 1, 1991? Discuss.

Questions 23 and 24 refer to the following fact pattern.

A woman who identified herself as Smith brought an auto into Carson's Auto Repair Shop ("CARS") for repairs. CARS completed the repairs for $5,000, which is a fair price for the work done and the parts and materials supplied. The day the repair work was completed, police informed CARS that the auto had been stolen by Smith and that Brown was the owner. Police took possession of the auto and returned it to Brown. CARS has not been paid and Smith has disappeared.

Brown did not have insurance on the auto. A week after recovering the auto, Brown sold it and transferred title to Jones for $8,000, the fair market value of the auto in its repaired condition. Brown deposited the $8,000 in his bank account, bringing the balance in the account to $22,000. A week after making that deposit, Brown withdrew $20,000 and lost it all gambling. One day later, Brown won $1,000 in the state lottery and deposited that amount into his bank account. No other changes in the account have taken place.

What remedies, if any, does CARS have:

23. Against Brown? Discuss.

24. Against Jones? Discuss.

Question 25 refers to the following fact pattern.

For the last three months, Jane has been demonstrating during business hours on the well-traveled public sidewalk in front of a five-story office building. She wears a "sandwich-board" sign over her shoulders and blows a whistle to attract further attention. On the sign, she has hand-lettered the following:

"Law Firm

of

Lawyer Services, Inc.

Is Crooked

The Firm Stole My Money!"

The law firm of Lawyer Services, Inc., is on the first floor of the building that is being picketed by Jane. The firm had represented Jane on a personal injury claim that was settled four months ago. Jane claimed that the firm wrongfully withheld $100 of a $200 fee that was supposed to have been paid to Dr. Dyer for the doctor's testimony on Jane's behalf at a deposition prior to settlement.

The law firm commenced a suit to enjoin Jane from further demonstration, claiming defamation and trade libel. The firm alleged that the injunction was needed to protect its reputation and to stop a continuing decrease in its earnings and in the number of walk-in clients.

At the hearing for the injunction, the law firm produced a cancelled check for the amount of $200 that was paid to Dr. Dyer. The doctor herself confirmed that she had received the full amount of her $200 fee. Jane offered no evidence other than her testimony that although she had spent her settlement money and was presently insolvent, she remained convinced that the firm had not paid Dr. Dyer the full $200.

25. Is the firm entitled to an injunction? Discuss.

1. What legal and equitable remedies does Al have against Betty? Discuss.

Al ("A") could sue Betty ("B") for breach of contract ("k"), or fraud.

Breach of contract

With respect to the breach of k action, B could contend that (1) A mutually agreed to rescind the transaction, (2) A suffered no monetary damages, since the $100,000 payment was returned to him, and (3) she could not reasonably foresee that A would lose money with respect to the other parcels of land which he purchased.

In rebuttal, however, A could argue that (1) the agreement to rescind was invalid, since it was procured by a fraud (i.e., B's representation that there was a defect in her title), (2) he did suffer damage by reason of the (i) diminished market value of the other land which he had purchased, and (ii) lost profits with respect to the shopping center, and (3) the losses A has or will incur on the other parcels was reasonably foreseeable, since A had advised B that he was buying 200 acres from other farmers for a "big project." Therefore, B should have recognized that if she withdrew her land (for which A had overpaid), A would be obliged to resell the other land he had purchased.

Based upon the foregoing, A can probably recover in breach of k for the diminished value of the other 200 acres that he purchased but not the lost shopping center profits. The latter are consequential damages, which were likely not foreseeable at the time the contract was entered into and are too speculative (it cannot reasonably be ascertained, had A operated the shopping center, how much profit would have been derived).

Fraud

One is liable in fraud where he deliberately misrepresents a material fact to another, upon which representation the latter justifiably relies to his detriment. Although B would contend that, since A's money was returned to him, there has been no detrimental reliance, this argument should fail (A has suffered losses with respect to the other acres which he purchased).

A would attempt to recover his actual losses to the extent such damages are reasonably susceptible of estimation. Thus, A should be able to recover for the losses suffered as a consequence of the diminished value of the other land he purchased but probably cannot recover for lost shopping center profits because these are too speculative.

A could also contend that a constructive trust in his favor should be imposed upon the $100,000 payment that B received from Claude ("C"). A constructive trust may be imposed where a person acquires property under circumstances where he would be unjustly enriched if permitted to retain it. To permit B to retain the proceeds received from effectuating a fraud upon A (i.e., advising him that she did not have good title to her land) would arguably be inequitable. Thus, A's constructive trust theory could be successful.

Additionally, punitive damages may be recovered for an intentional tort. Such damages seem appropriate in this instance since B's conduct (accepting a bribe to deprive someone of a prospective business advantage) is the type of action that should be discouraged. Note the punitive damages recovery would be based on Betty's act of fraud, not her breach of the contract.

2. What legal and equitable remedies does Al have against Claude? Discuss.

A could sue C for intentional interference with a (i) contractual relationship (the outstanding k that A had with B) and, (ii) prospective business advantage (the profits to be made from operation of the shopping center). Since there appears to be no privilege for C's actions, the assertion of these theories should be successful.

With respect to the former action, A could probably recover the difference between the price he paid for the other 200 acres and their present market price. A would, of course, be limited to a single recovery of this amount—be it from B or C. As to the lost profits, however, C could probably contend (as described above) that these damages are too speculative. A could also seek punitive damages for the foregoing intentional torts.

Since monetary damages would not make A whole with respect to the lost opportunity pertaining to the shopping center, he should request that the court issue a temporary restraining order (preventing C from completing and operating the shopping center) until the lawsuit is resolved. A would also request a mandatory injunction, requiring C to transfer his interest in the shopping center to A upon payment to C of his expenses with respect to the site (less any damages for which C is liable to A). It would be feasible to carry out this injunction, since the court could issue an order transferring the shopping center to A if C refused to execute the necessary documents. It is likely that this relief would be granted, since it represents the only means of putting A in the position he would have been in had C not induced B to breach the agreement with A.

3. What are Alice's rights and to what relief against Bob, if any, is she entitled? Discuss.

Alice ("A") could assert a negligence action against Bob ("B"), contending that the latter failed to act reasonably in permitting the ring to be left on the counter where another person might steal it. B could contend, however, that his failure to remove the ring from the counter was not the proximate cause of its loss, since the subsequent intentional theft and resale by Carl ("C") was an unforeseeable, intervening factor.

However, A could probably successfully argue in rebuttal that where the intervening, intentional criminal conduct was precisely the risk posed by the defendant's omission, proximate causation is satisfied. Thus, A could recover $14,000 (the amount that the ring was worth at the time of B's negligent conduct) from B, plus interest from the time it was converted.

4. What are Alice's rights and to what relief against Carl, if any, is she entitled? Discuss.

A could successfully contend that C converted her ring by removing it from B's counter and reselling it to Dan. A conversion occurs where the defendant intentionally causes a substantial interference with the plaintiff's use of, or ownership interest in, an item of personal property.

A would probably seek imposition of a constructive trust upon Blackacre ("B/A"). The imposition of a constructive trust is appropriate where the defendant has wrongfully acquired title to particular property when another has a superior equitable claim to the property.

Under the "tracing" doctrine, a plaintiff can follow identifiable property into a subsequent form. Since B/A is attributable to funds derived from the stolen ring, imposing a constructive trust upon B/A appears to be appropriate. However, some jurisdictions do not permit imposition of a constructive trust unless no adequate legal remedy is available to the plaintiff. If a constructive trust is imposed on the property, C would have the obligation, as trustee, to deliver it to A.

A might also attempt to impose a constructive trust upon C's savings account, at least to the extent of $600. Whether A would succeed depends upon the tracing methodology employed in this state and the balance (if any) which was in the account at the time the $2,000 deposit attributable to the ring was made.

If A is unable to obtain a constructive trust upon B/A or C's bank account, A could seek to obtain an equitable lien upon these assets. To impose such a lien (which could subsequently be foreclosed upon to satisfy the obligation owed by C to A): (1) the defendant must have misappropriated the plaintiff's property, (2) the plaintiff's property must be traceable to the asset upon which the plaintiff is seeking to impose the lien, and (3) retention of the property by the defendant would result in unjust enrichment. Since the foregoing requisites appear to be satisfied, an equitable lien would be appropriate. Again, however, some jurisdictions permit the imposition of an equitable lien only if the plaintiff's legal remedies are inadequate.

If equitable remedies are denied, under a conversion theory A would be entitled to recover the fair market value of the item on the date upon which it was appropriated by C, plus interest thereon until the date of payment. A might also recover punitive damages, since C's actions constitute fraudulent behavior that should be discouraged.

5. What are Alice's rights and to what relief against Dan, if any, is she entitled? Discuss.

Dan "D" committed a conversion of the ring (i.e., he purchased it with the intent of owning the item), even though he did so innocently. Thus, while D is liable for the fair market value of the ring at the time he acquired it, plus interest thereon until the date such payment was made, punitive damages would not be possible in this instance.

Alternatively, A could assert an action for replevin (sometimes also called "claim and delivery") against D. Pursuant to this theory, A has the right to recover the ring back from D, plus damages in an amount equal to the reasonable rental value of it for the period of time during which the item was in D's possession. Note a good faith purchaser for value from a thief does not acquire good title and remains liable for either the good (replevin) or the value of the good (conversion).

6. What are the rights and remedies, if any, of Peter against Al? Discuss.

Since Bret ("B") put up the billboards after receiving permission from Al ("A"), an initial question is whether A had the right to authorize construction of the billboards (if A had no right to erect the billboards, then he would have had no authority to permit B to do so).

Ordinarily, a landowner may use his land in any manner whatsoever. There is no indication from the facts that A and Peter ("P") had ever entered into an agreement whereby A would restrict his use of Blackacre. In most states, a negative easement for light cannot be created by implication. Thus, there is no reason why A could not authorize B to erect the billboards.

P might attempt to sue A in nuisance (i.e., that A has engaged in conduct that causes a non-trespassory, substantial, and unreasonable interference with P's right to enjoy Restview) or wrongfully interfering with a prospective business advantage (presumably, Restview will have fewer customers if the countryside view is impaired and sunlight into the dining room diminished). However, the erection and maintenance of billboards probably does not constitute an unreasonable interference with P's use of Restview, since B (via A) has a right to use Blackacre in a commercially profitable manner. There would also appear to be nothing wrongful in A's conduct (one is not ordinarily constrained from using their land in a manner that will result in a neighbor's land becoming less valuable). Thus, these torts appear to be absent.

If, however, A and P had agreed to and recorded a negative easement (and therefore A did not have the right to authorize construction of the billboards), P could probably obtain a mandatory injunction to have them removed. A mandatory injunction is appropriate where monetary damages will be inadequate. Since it would be difficult for P to prove with reasonable certainty what his monetary losses would be as a consequence of the billboards (many prospective customers might not come to Restview, and those who did, might never return, etc.), a mandatory injunction seems appropriate.

A could, in rebuttal, argue laches. Since P was presumably aware of the billboards as they were being constructed and has waited two years to threaten suit, he might be deemed to have delayed an unreasonably long period of time. A's argument is buttressed by the significant expense ($25,000) incurred by B in the construction of the billboards. Again, A should prevail.

Assuming P can prevail in a tort action and monetary damages are the only remedy available to P, P probably would have to prove that specific persons decided against coming to Restview because of the billboards. Some courts, however, would permit P to recover the difference between Restview's past profitability and the lower income derived after the billboards were constructed (assuming it can be shown that the diminished attendance was most probably the result of the impaired view of the countryside).

In summary, however, P probably has no rights against A.

7. What are the rights and remedies, if any, of Bret against Al? Discuss.

If A commenced an action against B to remove the billboards, A would contend that, since B paid nothing for the right to install the billboards (i.e., there was no consideration), the former could order the latter to remove them. A might also argue that, since B was A's son-in-law, B should have realized that A did not intend a contractual-type arrangement (and therefore that A could withdraw his consent at any time). Lastly, A would argue that the purported agreement is too indefinite to be enforceable (nothing was said as to how long the billboards could remain, how large they could be, where they could be placed, etc.).

In rebuttal, B could contend that (1) promissory estoppel precludes A from asserting the lack of consideration (since he relied upon A's statement to his detriment in constructing the billboards at a cost of $25,000), (2) although they were related, each looked upon the transaction as being legally binding (they had prolonged discussions and consulted a lawyer as to the exact granting language that was necessary), and (3) any indefiniteness with respect to the arrangement could be cured by implied terms (i.e., the billboards could remain for a reasonable period of time, they could be placed anywhere upon Blackacre, the billboards had to be reasonable in size, etc.). Given the fact that A apparently raised no objection to the billboards during the initial two years of their existence, B should be successful upon the foregoing arguments.

Assuming the conveyance from A to B was something other than a license (which is a personal property interest and not subject to the Statute of Frauds), A might also contend that any purported agreement with B is unenforceable by reason of the Statute of Frauds (where an interest in land is transferred, the conveyance must be reflected in a writing that contains the essential terms and is signed by the grantor). However, promissory estoppel will also permit B to avoid the application of the Statute of Frauds.

It therefore appears that A has no right to remove B's signs.

Assuming, however, A removed B's signs, B would probably seek a mandatory injunction to have them restored and damages. The billboards advertised a business operated by B, B would assert that an injunction is proper because monetary damages would be inadequate (it would be impossible to prove how many additional customers would have come to B's business premises, and how much they would have purchased).

In rebuttal, A might contend that the relationship between A and B was one of licensor/licensee. Ordinarily, a license is revocable at any time (although the licensor is liable for damages that the licensee incurs as a result of the loss of the license). However, where a license is coupled with an interest or is commercial in nature, some courts consider it irrevocable. Since B expended $25,000 and the signs probably advertised B's business, it is likely that B's license would be deemed to be either coupled with an interest or commercial in nature, and therefore irrevocable.

Assuming B is restricted to damages, the traditional rule is that one can recover only for specific transactions which failed to occur by reason of the misconduct in question. Modernly, some courts have permitted the plaintiff to recover for general business losses (i.e., the difference between B's usual business profits and the diminished amount for the period of time during which the billboards would have been on A's property).

In summary, however, B can probably compel A to refrain from removing the signs or to restore them (if they have already been removed).

8. What rights and remedies, if any, does Cal have? Discuss.

Reformation

An initial issue is "can the contract be reformed to reflect the purchase of both Blackacre ("B/A") and Whiteacre ("W/A")?" Under the parol evidence rule, evidence that is inconsistent with an integration is not admissible. Since the writing pertains only to B/A, Sam ("S") might argue that Cal ("C") is precluded from introducing proof that the original transaction also covered W/A.

However, an integrated contract can ordinarily be reformed to reflect the parties' actual agreement, where there is "clear and convincing" evidence that a term was inadvertently omitted. C could probably satisfy this burden of proof, since (1) the contract alludes to "... 20 acres, more or less" (it is unlikely that the land involved would be only about one-half as large as anticipated), (2) at the time the contract was made, land in the area was only worth $1,000 per parcel (it is unlikely that Bob would have agreed to pay twice the then fair market value of the land), and (3) S may have advised his attorney that the transaction was to cover both B/A and W/A (the lawyer presumably overlooked the fact that the final agreement did not reflect his client's instructions). Thus, the contract would probably be reformed to cover B/A and W/A.

Constructive condition precedent

S could contend that payment of the entire purchase price was a condition precedent to his performance. While there was no express condition precedent to this effect, there is a constructive (i.e., implied) condition precedent that where the performances of each party are to occur concurrently, each side's tender is a condition precedent to the other side's obligation to perform. Since delivery of the deeds and payment of the $10,000 balance could happen concurrently, C's failure to deliver the entire balance arguably released S from his duty to deliver the deeds.

Abatement

C could argue in rebuttal that where a buyer learns that land that is to be conveyed to him is less than anticipated by the parties, the purchaser (if he chooses to consummate the transaction) is entitled to an abatement in the purchase price equal to the diminished value of the property. Since S owns 15% less acreage than indicated in the (1) assessor's records, and (2) contract (the parcels aggregated "20 acres, more or less"), the $7,000 tender was appropriate.

S could respond, however, that (1) the acreage alluded to in the contract was an approximation, (2) he is not responsible for misstatements in the public record made by the county assessor, (3) C should have performed his own survey to verify the precise acreage being conveyed, and (4) since C was aware that W/A embodied only 7 acres prior to the closing date and (apparently) made no effort to reconcile this variance with S, C cannot unilaterally determine the proper amount owing to S at the eleventh hour. S's arguments should be successful.

Lapse

S could next argue that since the due date for payment of the balance has passed, his obligation to perform has expired. However, assuming the closing date did not occur too long ago, C is probably not yet in material breach of the agreement (there was no "time is of the essence" clause). Thus, C should either (1) tender $10,000 to S, but reserve his right to sue for abatement under quasi-contract principles, or (2) immediately commence an action for specific performance, coupled with a request for an abatement in the purchase price.

Quasi-contract

If C is unable to tender the entire purchase price to S or commence a lawsuit, he could recover the $10,000 paid to S one year ago under a quasi-contract theory (i.e., S would be unjustly enriched if allowed to retain the land and the initial $10,000 payment too). However, if the contract contained a valid liquidated damages clause, S may be able to retain the original down payment, as long as the court does not find the provision to be a penalty.

C v. Bob

It is unlikely that C has any rights against Bob. C is probably charged with notice of the terms contained in the contract which was assigned to him.

9. Can Andy obtain an injunction to prevent the Corp-Endrun merger? Discuss.

Theory of liability

Ben, Carl, and Dave have attempted to avoid Andy's veto power by accepting a proposal to merge with Rich's corporation. In effect, Ben, Carl, and Dave are attempting to avoid the super majority (80 percent) voting restrictions, the preemptive rights restrictions, and the cumulative voting requirements in Corp's articles. Andy will claim this is a breach of the fiduciary duty of good faith owed by the majority shareholders (Ben, Carl, and Dave together own 75 percent of the shares) to Andy, the minority shareholder.

Right to injunctive relief

Assuming that Andy can show a breach of fiduciary duty, he must also demonstrate the requirements for injunctive relief in tort. In this regard, inadequacy of the legal remedy and the equitable defense of unclean hands may pose difficulties for awarding injunctive relief.

Inadequate legal remedy. In order to obtain injunctive relief, Andy must show that the legal remedy (here damages) is inadequate. Damages are probably speculative due to the difficulty of ascertaining monetary damage in case the merger is approved (loss of interest payments could be quantified but diminution in voting strength, corporate control, etc., would be very speculative). Secondly, a 25 percent block of shares in a closely held corporation may be similar to a unique chattel or real property, which cannot be compensated for with money.

Unclean hands. One seeking injunctive relief will be denied that remedy if the applicant has committed any wrongful or inequitable conduct injuring the defendant in the same transaction or dispute for which the injunctive relief is sought. The facts indicate that Andy purchased the high interest note for his own economic benefit. Additionally, Lender approached Andy as treasurer for Corp offering to sell the note and Andy took advantage of his corporate office to the detriment of Corp. For these reasons, and Andy's possible breach of fiduciary duty, a court may deny Andy the injunctive relief requested.

10. What are Homeowners' rights and remedies against Bob? Discuss.

Damages. An action for damages may be precluded by the fact that land values in the area may actually increase if a shopping center is built. However, if the nuisance is established, Homeowners should be able to recover for the loss of use and enjoyment of their property. It should be noted that if the shopping center is deemed to be a public nuisance (interference with the rights of the community at large), then they will have to show unique injury in order to recover. Many courts will refuse to award damages for violation of an implied reciprocal servitude because of its origins in equity. Modern courts do not feel so constrained and will award the damages remedy if all the prima facie elements exist.

Injunction. Homeowners' preferred remedy will be to enjoin construction of the proposed shopping center. To do so they will need to establish the following elements:

Tort or breach of contract. Here, the tort of interference with real property or nuisance would be the basis for injunctive relief. Similarly, the violation of the implied reciprocal servitude could be the basis for the remedy.

Inadequate legal remedy. Money damages would be inadequate here because the injury is to Homeowners' enjoyment of their property, which would be difficult to measure and should continue indefinitely.

Feasibility. The court would be able to enforce an injunction here by holding Bob in contempt if he did not stop building.

Property right. Homeowners' property rights are involved here.

Balancing. Homeowners will have to show that the injury to them is greater if the shopping center is allowed than the injury to Bob if the center is enjoined. Here, Bob may have paid a substantial premium for the land because of the possibility of commercial development. If the nuisance theory is used, the court will also look at the utility of Bob's shopping center versus the harm to Homeowners. The increase in jobs and shopping services may be enough to tip the balance in favor of the shopping center under a nuisance theory. With respect to the violation of the servitude, the court will consider the justifiable expectation of Bob and the adverse effect an injunction will have on his interests.

Defenses. The changed circumstances defense has previously been discussed. Laches is not available since the Homeowners registered their objections promptly. No other defenses appear to be applicable. Assuming that Homeowners can prevail on the balancing element, injunctive relief should be granted.

11. How should the court rule on the following grounds urged in support of the motion to dismiss? "Even if the complaint states a cause of action, the damages sought cannot be recovered by any theory suggested by the facts alleged." Discuss.

Proff will want to bring actions for damages under both tort and contract theories.

Tort Damages

Compensatory. Provided that the jurisdiction recognizes a negligent misrepresentation theory, Proff can recover compensatory damages, which will include all damages proximately caused by Flyright's negligence. Here, Proff should be able to recover the $10,000 lecture fee if he can establish that the lecture fee loss was a foreseeable consequence of receiving improper flight information. Courts are more willing to find damages to be foreseeable in tort than in contract actions, but Proff may have difficulty here because he never told the Flyright employee why he had to be at his destination by 3:00 p.m. If the court finds that Proff's loss of the lecture fee was unforeseeable, then he wiIl be limited to recovery of the price of the ticket.

Punitives. Punitive damages are generally unavailable absent a showing that the defendant's conduct is intentional or reckless. No facts justify such a finding here.

Contract Damages

Proff most certainly would be entitled to receive his money back for the price of the ticket. Restitution is available to a contract breach recipient. However, the lost lecture fee would be considered consequential damages, which must be shown to be foreseeable to the breaching party at the time the contract is entered into (*Hadley v. Baxendale*). As discussed above, the reason for Proff's flight was never explained to Flyright. It was not foreseeable to Flyright that their failure to give proper flight time information to Proff would result in the loss of the lecture fee. Proff cannot recover this fee in a breach of contract action. In addition, punitive damages are not available in contract.

12. Is the following ruling of the trial judge (who sat without a jury) correct? "Cobb had breached the contract but could recover $8,000 on his claim." Discuss.

On balance, the court probably did not err under in concluding that Cobb's unilateral mistake is no defense to enforcement of the contract.

Liability theory: Contract

Formation. Owen and Cobb entered into a written bilateral contract whereby Cobb promised to remodel Owen's house and Owen promised to pay $20,000. Cobb only completed 50 percent of the work, then refused to proceed at the contract price because of his bookkeeper's $4,000 mathematical error in calculating labor costs. Whether Cobb's refusal to complete the job constitutes a breach depends on whether his unilateral mistake is a valid defense to enforcement of the contract.

Unilateral mistake

Traditional rule. The traditional rule is that a party such as Cobb who makes a unilateral mistake may rescind the contract only if the other party knew or should have known about the mistake. Here, there is no indication that Owen actually knew or should have known about Cobb's miscalculation. Owen did not initially seek bids from other contractors, so he had no notice that Cobb's bid for $20,000 was suspiciously low.

Modern rule. A minority of modern jurisdictions would permit Cobb to rescind the deal if he could show that the hardship of enforcement on him would substantially outweigh the detriment to Owen of rescission. If the court enforced the contract for the original price, Cobb's miscalculation by $4,000 (20 percent of the contract price) probably would mean he would lose money on the deal. On the other hand, Owen had to pay an additional $5,000 over the contract price to another contractor to get what he bargained for.

Performance

Since Cobb has no valid defense to enforcement of the contract against him, did his obligation to remodel Owen's house mature into an absolute duty which he then breached when he refused to finish the job?

Condition. The only condition to Cobb's obligation to perform was Owen's payment of $2,000 when the contract was signed. Owen paid Cobb the money, and thus this condition precedent to Cobb's obligation to remodel Owen's house was satisfied and Cobb had an absolute duty to do the job.

There was also a constructive condition precedent to Owen's obligation to pay the $18,000 balance of the contract price to Cobb, i.e., Cobb's completion of the job. Since

Cobb never completed the job, he cannot argue that Owen somehow was in breach and should pay him damages.

Discharge. Cobb may assert that the increased cost of the job discharged his duty to perform through the doctrine of severe impracticability or commercial frustration. However, his bookkeeper's mathematical error is not the kind of unforeseen supervening event or change in circumstances that would justify releasing Cobb from his absolute duty to perform, and the hardship of the increased cost is simply not an appropriate ground for discharge.

Breach. Cobb had an absolute duty to remodel Owen's house. When he refused to finish the other 50 percent of the job at the original contract price, this constituted a willful material breach of the contract.

Remedies

Cobb's breach of the contract will entitle Owen, the nonbreaching party, to a remedy in damages. Even though Cobb is the breaching party, moreover, he also may be entitled to recover something in restitution.

Cobb's breach and $8,000 recovery

Breach. The court was correct in ruling that Cobb had breached the contract as explained above.

Cobb's $8,000 recovery—Restitution. Where a party has not substantially performed (here Cobb only completed 50 percent of the job), and where the contract is not divisible, the breachor still may recover the value for the benefit conferred on the other party to prevent unjust enrichment. This recovery is offset by any damages caused by the breach. The excess of the value to Owen of Cobb's incomplete performance over the damages caused to Owen by that incomplete performance may be returned to Cobb as restitution for his efforts. In order to calculate this amount, both Rulings 1 and 2 must be taken into account (see below).

Willful breach. Some jurisdictions deny restitution entirely to a party whose breach of contract is willful and amounts to bad faith. In these jurisdictions, the court would have erred in awarding Cobb anything if the court found his breach was willful and in bad faith.

Value of benefit conferred on Owen. Assuming a court would permit restitution, Cobb could recover $8,000 as the reasonable value of his performance. The original contract price was $20,000. Cobb completed 50 percent of the job—$10,000 worth—and had already been paid $2,000. Note a court is not bound by the contract price and could find the reasonable value of Cobb's performance was less than the contract price. Thus, Cobb may be able to recover $8,000 (minus the offset of damages to Owen, discussed below).

13. Is the following ruling of the trial judge (who sat without a jury) correct? "Cobb's recovery would be offset by $5,000, as damages owing to Owen based on Cobb's breach of the contract." Discuss.

The value conferred on Owen must take into account the damages caused to him by Cobb's breach.

Owen's duty to mitigate

As soon as Owen received notice of Cobb's breach, he had a duty to avoid further costs and losses by seeking substitute performance. He did this by obtaining bids from two other contractors and accepting the lower bid.

Expectation damages

Owen is entitled to recover as expectation damages the difference between the cost of completion and the original contract price. Owen ended up paying $25,000 for the remodeling job ($10,000 to Cobb plus $15,000 to the second contractor), which is $5,000 over the original contract price of $20,000.

Replacement of paneling. Cobb may argue that instead of Owen recovering $5,000, he should only get $3,500 ($5,000 minus the $1,500 it cost to replace the paneling), plus any diminution in value caused by the lighter paneling. However, it appears that the court was correct in awarding Owen the full $5,000, which included the replacement cost of the paneling. The $1,500 spent does not seem disproportionate to the benefit conferred on Owen in having the type and quality of paneling he ordered. For one thing, the paneling was in a living area (the family room) where personal taste is a valid concern. For another, the paneling Cobb used was apparently not just a different type from the paneling Owen had ordered, but of a lower quality, i.e., a "much lighter weight."

Cobb should probably be awarded a net of $3,000 ($8,000 to Cobb minus $5,000 to Owen) in restitution to prevent unjust enrichment to Owen.

14. Is the following ruling of the trial judge (who sat without a jury) correct? "Owen could not recover any amount based on the liquidated damages clause in the contract." Discuss.

The original contract contained a liquidated damages provision whereby the amount Owen owed Cobb would be reduced by $500 for each month, or part thereof, of delay past the November 1, completion date. The job was completed on December 1, one month late. Whether the provision should be enforced as a valid liquidated damages clause or stricken as a void penalty depends on: (1) whether damages were difficult to ascertain at the time the contract was formed, and (2) whether the parties made a reasonable estimate of the damages. If both of these requirements are present, the clause will be enforced.

Difficult to ascertain

This was a residential remodeling job where the owner continued to live in the house, so delay damages would be for inconvenience rather than for the extra cost of renting elsewhere during the delay. Since it is difficult to put a money value on inconveniences damages, damages appear to have been difficult to ascertain, thus satisfying the first requirement.

Reasonable estimate

It is hard to tell whether $500 per month was a reasonable estimate of damages, but it seems excessive if the delay was only one day (which would still be $500 since the clause stated "each month, or part thereof"). Although traditionally the reasonableness is judged at the time the contract was made, modern courts may look at the actual harm after the breach. While the clause may have been judged as an unreasonable estimate under the traditional view, $500 for an actual full month of delay seems reasonable and should be upheld.

Conclusion

The court should have enforced the liquidated damages clause and awarded Owen $500.

15. What are Paul's rights and remedies, if any, against Dan? Discuss.

The facts state that Dan "resolved to do what he could to hinder the operation of Paul's new restaurant." After this apparently clear-cut statement of tortious intent, Dan acted to hinder Paul's relationships with: (1) Chef, (2) Meatco, and (3) Seller. For Paul to recover from Dan, first he must establish theories of liability for what Dan did.

Inducing breach of Chef's employment contract

Liability—Inducing breach of contract. This economic tort requires a volitional act by defendant, done with the requisite intent, which causes a third person to breach an existing contract with plaintiff.

Here, a third person, Chef, had an existing employment contract with Paul to head up the kitchen staff of Paul's new restaurant. Dan actively caused Chef to terminate his employment with Paul by offering to double Chef's salary and by threatening to "make it difficult" for Chef to get his next job if he did not quit his job with Paul. Under the facts, it is clear that Dan intended to cause Chef to breach his contract with Paul.

However, the Chef-Paul agreement allowed either party to terminate the relationship on thirty days' notice. If Chef gave the requisite thirty days' notice to terminate his relationship with Paul, there has been no breach and Dan's conduct would not be actionable except in a jurisdiction that protects prospective contractual relationships.

Privilege. Even assuming that Chef quit without notice, Dan may still avoid liability if he can prove the defense of privilege. This requires that defendant's activity was undertaken for a justifiable purpose and that defendant utilized justifiable methods to achieve that purpose.

Dan would argue that he was acting to protect his own existing financial interest in the ten restaurants he owns that would be adversely affected by competition from Paul's new restaurant. Even if this was a justifiable purpose, at least part of Dan's methods are questionable. Dan used threats of blackballing Chef in the industry to induce Chef to leave Paul's employment, which goes beyond the usual justifiable inducements for an employee to change jobs, such as offering to increase salary. Because of Dan's threat bordering on extortion, his privilege defense likely will fall, entitling Paul to remedies against Dan for inducing breach of his contract with Chef.

Remedies

Damages. Paul may recover from Dan all compensatory damages resulting from Dan's tortious conduct so long as the damages are foreseeable, certain, and unavoidable. This may include the additional cost of hiring a substitute employee for the remaining term of Chef's contract. (Paul has a duty to mitigate his damages.) But this raises Paul's first problem with his damage recovery. Because of the thirty-day notice provision, probably thirty days would be the full extent of the contract period for which Paul could recover. Chef could have left Paul's employment after this short period without being in breach of the contract, thus requiring Paul to hire a replacement anyway.

Also, any lost profits Paul could claim may properly be restricted to this same short period. As to lost profits, though, Paul may have difficulty proving his damages with reasonable certainty. Because his restaurant is still new, there probably is not a sufficient economic track record upon which Paul could rely to prove any alleged lost profits with the requisite certainty.

Paul would also seek to recover for the damage done to his reputation in the restaurant community, but this may be a problem since his theory of recovery is inducing breach of contract, and not defamation.

Even if Paul was awarded only nominal damages, though, he may be able to get an accompanying award of punitive damages if Dan is found to have acted with a purpose to vex or harass Paul. Given Dan's stated intent to "do what he could to hinder the operation of Paul's restaurant," punitive damages may be appropriate here to punish Dan and to deter others from engaging in such conduct.

Injunction. To show that money damages were inadequate, Paul may also argue that Chef's skill, knowledge, and reputation were such that his services were unique, thus entitling Paul to injunctive relief. Because this is a personal services contract and Chef is not a party to the lawsuit, no mandatory injunction would be available to force Chef to continue working for Paul. And while a prohibitory order would be feasible, prohibiting Dan from employing Chef himself, there would be the same 30-day time limit on such an injunction (see discussion above).

Interference with Meatco food supply contract

Liability—Inducing breach of contract. Paul may assert the same liability theory discussed above for Dan's disruption of Paul's food supply contract with Meatco. Paul and Meatco had a three-year contract under which Meatco was under a duty to deliver high quality meat each week to Paul. This is a contract involving the sale of goods and is governed by the Uniform Commercial Code. There is no problem with the lack of a quantity term or a price—this appears to be a valid requirements contract under which Meatco has undertaken to supply Paul with his weekly meat requirements and Paul has agreed to pay for the meat delivered.

Dan interfered with this contract by writing Meatco that if it continued to supply Paul with meat, Dan would not continue to deal with Meatco when his existing contract ended in two weeks. Dan's letter constituted a volitional act done with the intent to cause Meatco to breach its existing contract with Paul.

Privilege. Dan may seek to avoid liability by asserting that his conduct was privileged. As discussed above, Dan's purpose may have been justified if it was privileged to protect the existing economic interest he had in his own restaurants. Here Dan may argue it was also to protect his existing economic interest in his own contract with Meatco. However, there is nothing to suggest that Meatco could not adequately supply both Paul and Dan with meat, which would mean that Dan's real purpose was to throttle the competition posed by Paul's new restaurant, rather than to protect his own meat supply for his restaurants.

As for justifiable methods, Dan may have a better chance of prevailing here where his "threat" was refusal to deal, rather than exerting his influence to destroy someone's future job opportunities if they did not cooperate.

Assuming Dan's conduct was not privileged, Paul would be entitled to remedies.

Remedies

Damages. As compensatory damages, Paul would seek to recover the difference between the contract price and market price of comparable meat (or whatever he actually ended up paying for his meat requirements if he exercised his right to cover). The same problems of speculation (see above) creep into the calculation of these damages due to the newness of Paul's business, as do the same problems with damage to Paul's reputation. Paul may seek punitive damages as well, if he can prove malice.

Injunction. Paul may argue that his legal remedy is inadequate due to the certainty problem discussed above. He may request equitable relief in the form of an injunction, but there are several problems with this. First, in all likelihood there are comparable meat suppliers, meaning that Paul's legal remedy may be adequate. In addition, the court has no jurisdiction over Meatco in this action anyway, and therefore cannot order it to supply Paul's meat requirements. At most the court could prohibit Dan from getting his supplies from Meatco, but this is unlikely.

Interference with prospective advantage: Seller's acceptance of Dan's offer

Liability—Interference with prospective economic advantage. Because there was no existing contract between Seller and Paul, Paul cannot recover against Dan for inducing breach of contract with Seller. Paul's theory of liability here would be that by offering Seller a much higher price for his house than that offered by Paul, Dan interfered with Paul's expectancy of economic benefit from buying Seller's house.

Privilege. The privilege defense with regard to this tort is much broader than with inducing breach of contract. Dan would be given much greater latitude to protect his own financial interest, including Dan's expected (rather than existing) economic advantage. Although Dan's motive was to divert Paul's attention from operating his restaurant, his ultimate purpose still appears to have been to protect his own restaurant business. And since there is nothing unusual or improper in outbidding another prospective house buyer in what appears to be a tight housing market, Dan probably will not be liable for offering Seller a higher price, whatever his motive.

Personal versus commercial purpose. Paul's other problem here is that the purchase of a home is more personal than commercial. While the Chef and Meatco relationships with Paul were clearly for business purposes, the Seller's relationship (to the extent one existed) was more for Paul's personal benefit. This may make it even more unlikely that Paul could hold Dan liable for any kind of economic tort for outbidding him on the house.

16. What are Howard's rights and remedies, if any? Discuss.

Howard may recover damages to return him to the condition he occupied prior to the occurrence of the nuisance and/or trespass.

Nuisance damages

Recovery may be available to "make plaintiff whole" as long as the damages are foreseeable, certain, and unavoidable. Traditionally, damages for nuisance were measured by the loss of use and enjoyment of plaintiff's property, the discomfort and annoyance to plaintiff caused by the nuisance, and any cost associated with seeking abatement of the nuisance. Here, Howard may recover for the damage caused to his lawn by the chemicals burning it, and for the discomfort and annoyance caused by the noise and dust. However, under this traditional view, Howard's losses would be limited to those incurred up to the time of trial.

Permanent nuisance. In order to avoid a multiplicity of lawsuits, modern jurisdictions may also allow recovery for future invasions under the doctrine of permanent nuisance. In these jurisdictions, if Howard can show that the nuisance cannot be or is unlikely to be abated, he also may recover for the diminution in the value of his land caused by the nuisance.

Trespass

Alternatively, Howard may recover compensatory damages for Refin's trespass (its chemicals entry onto Howard's land). Howard could only recover punitive damages to punish Refin and to deter others from such conduct if he can show that Refin's conduct was "willful, wanton, or malicious." There is nothing to suggest that the invasion of plaintiff's land was done with the requisite malice, precluding recovery of punitive damages.

Injunctive relief

What Howard really would like is for the court to compel Refin to stop its smelter activities that create the nuisance. Since he can show an underlying tort, such a prohibitory injunction may be granted if he can satisfy the following special requirements for this equitable relief.

Inadequate legal remedy. The legal remedy of damages is inadequate here for several reasons. First, since Howard's real property interest is involved, the traditional "uniqueness" of real property is sufficient justification to find money damages inadequate. Second, Refin's ongoing smelter activities constitute a continuing nuisance (probably requiring repetitive suits for damages) and may cause irreparable injury (to the health and safety of the residents). These factors also make Howard's legal recovery inadequate.

Feasible decree. There is no problem with the feasibility of enforcing the prohibitory injunction requested here. If Refin does not stop the activities enjoined, the court can hold Refin in contempt.

Balancing of hardships. Although the analysis of liability under nuisance involves a balancing of interests, many courts engage in a second balancing of harm versus utility to determine whether to issue the injunction. This time the focus is on whether defendant's activity is reasonable, rather than whether the interference with plaintiff's use and enjoyment is reasonable. The same factors described above under nuisance would be considered.

If the court determines that the overall benefit to the community (e.g., jobs created, other economic benefits) outweighs the harm (e.g., noise, dust, threat of chemical contamination), the court may deny the injunction and leave Howard with an award of damages. On the other hand, if the court finds the harm greater than the utility, it may enjoin Refin's nuisance-making activity.

Some courts refuse to perform a second balancing in nuisance cases. They regard nuisance as a willful invasion and grant injunctive relief as a matter of course once nuisance has been found.

Property right. Although many modern courts have abolished this requirement, there is no problem satisfying it here anyway since Howard's real property is involved.

Defenses. There are no facts to suggest that any of the equitable defenses, e.g., laches, unclean hands, apply to Howard here. It should be noted that Howard's "coming to the nuisance" would be a factor in the court's balancing of the equities (harm v. benefit) done to determine if the smelter is a nuisance and if an injunction should be issued. It is not an absolute defense to an action for a nuisance.

Conclusion

The court should issue the requested injunction if, on balance, it finds the continuing harm caused by Refin's activities to outweigh the benefits to the community. If the benefits outweigh the harm, the court should refuse to issue the injunction but order Refin to pay Howard damages.

17. What are Insco's rights and remedies against The Red Cross? Discuss.

Liability theory: Conversion

A conversion is a volitional, intentional act by the defendant that causes the destruction or serious and substantial interference with the plaintiff's chattel. Henry embezzled $50,000 from Insco. He donated $5,000 of these funds to the Red Cross. By accepting the money, the Red Cross committed a voluntary, intentional act sufficient for conversion because keeping the donation was a serious interference with Insco's possession of their money. The fact that the Red Cross was unaware of Henry's embezzlement is no defense. Conversion does not require that the defendant intend or realize the legal significance of the act, only an intent to do the act, which results in a serious and substantial interference. The elements for conversion are met.

Remedies: Damages or restitution

Plaintiff may generally elect to receive either damages or restitution as a remedy for conversion. Insco's damages would be measured as the fair market value of the property at the time of conversion, plus consequential damages. Here, that would allow Insco to recover $5,000 plus interest for loss of use of the money.

In restitution, a plaintiff may obtain return of the property plus damages for loss of use. The fact that the Red Cross is an "innocent" converter is no defense to these remedies. As a donee, the Red Cross is not a bona fide purchaser. Insco will receive $5,000 plus interest, whether it seeks damages or restitution from the Red Cross.

18. What are Insco's rights and remedies against the funds in Henry's savings account with Bank? Discuss.

Liability theory: Conversion

Henry's act of embezzlement is also a conversion. The problem is that Henry deposited $25,000 of Insco's money in a bank account that also contained $20,000 of his own money, and then made subsequent withdrawals and deposits from the account.

Remedies: Equitable lien and constructive trust

When the defendant wrongfully obtains the plaintiff's money and commingles that money with the defendant's own money, plaintiff may seek to impose an equitable lien or constructive trust over the combined fund.

Equitable lien. Insco may seek to have the court impose an equitable lien on the $15,000 in the account that remained after Henry withdrew the $30,000, which he lost at the racetrack. Regardless of the tracing method adopted by the jurisdiction, (e.g., first-in, first-out, defendant's funds first, plaintiff's advantage, etc.), Insco should be able to show that since Henry had $20,000 of his own money in the account prior to adding the embezzled funds, the $20,000 of the $30,000 withdrawn should be considered to be Henry's own money. Thus, the $15,000 remaining in the account after the withdrawal rightfully belongs to Insco and should be subject to an equitable lien in Insco's favor.

Constructive trust. Insco may also seek to impose a constructive trust over the $15,000 in lottery winnings Henry deposited in the account. When a defendant knowingly uses plaintiff's money to purchase other property, the court will impose a constructive trust as to a pro rata share (measured by the proportion of the commingled fund comprised of plaintiff's money) of property purchased with money from the fund. However, Henry used his own earnings to purchase the winning lottery ticket, not money in the commingled savings account. Thus, Insco is not entitled to a constructive trust over the $15,000 in lottery winnings in the account.

19. What are Insco's rights and remedies against Susan's certificate of deposit? Discuss.

Remedies

Constructive trust. Insco should instead seek to impose a constructive trust over the proceeds of the insurance policy invested in the certificate of deposit. Using a constructive trust, a plaintiff who can trace the converted property through changes in form (here, from a life insurance policy premium to its death benefit to a certificate of deposit). The majority of courts limit the constructive trust in a life insurance situation to the value of the converted funds used to pay the insurance premiums, in this case $10,000. A court might include interest on the $10,000.

Equitable lien. Insco could instead seek an equitable lien upon the certificate of deposit because it was purchased with proceeds of the life insurance policy purchased with Insco's money. However, an equitable lien does not entitle the plaintiff to recover any increase in value caused by use of the converted funds. Thus, Insco would only have a claim as to $10,000 of the $100,000 certificate of deposit if it elects to seek an equitable lien.

20. What are Insco's rights and remedies against the personal property in Henry's estate? Discuss.

Liability theory: Conversion

As discussed previously, Henry's embezzlement of Insco's funds will also constitute the tort of conversion. Moreover, Henry's estate be liable because nearly all states have enacted some type of survival statute, which permits a plaintiff to recover from the estate of the tortfeasor.

Remedies

Insco is unable to determine what happened to the other $10,000 taken by Henry. Thus, it may be able to seek damages or restitution by looking to the $10,000 of personal property in Henry's estate.

Damages. Although Insco's equitable lien and constructive trust claims are secured claims, entitled to priority over other creditors, Insco's remaining damages claims are unsecured and will not be given priority over any other claims against Henry's estate. Thus, unless there are no other superior claims, Insco will not be able to force a sale of the personal property to satisfy any damages judgment it may obtain against Henry's estate.

Restitution or equitable relief. Insco will not be able to obtain any restitution or equitable relief because it cannot establish that any of the embezzled funds were used to acquire any of the personal property in the estate. Thus, at least, Insco has an unsecured damages claim against Henry's estate.

21. Is Peter entitled to a preliminary injunction against ABC restraining it from proceeding with construction based on the changed building plans? Discuss.

A preliminary injunction is a temporary order designed to maintain the status quo between the parties pending a final decision on the merits of the cause of action. A party seeking a preliminary injunction (i.e., Peter) must establish all the requirements of injunctive relief in order to obtain this remedy. Those elements will be discussed below.

Underlying cause of action. In order to obtain any form of injunctive relief, a party must establish that some form of wrongful conduct has occurred entitling that party to injunctive relief. Generally, this requires establishment of a tort or interference with a property right. Here, Peter will assert that ABC's refusal to honor the lease agreement constitutes an interference with Peter's property rights under the lease.

Inadequate remedy at law. An injunction will not issue unless the legal remedy is inadequate. This element is satisfied for several reasons. First, real property is generally considered unique such that an injunction should issue to protect the interest rather than forcing a plaintiff to accept money as compensation. Second, money damages will not fully compensate Peter if the preliminary injunction is not issued. Here, Peter's damages would be measured by the lost profits resulting from ABC's refusal to accommodate his sporting goods store in the new ABC mall. Even though Peter is an experienced sporting goods merchant in the same city, it would be difficult to ascertain the amount of profits he would have earned in the new mall during the period of the preliminary injunction. Third, and most importantly, if Peter is unsuccessful in obtaining a preliminary injunction halting construction, it is highly unlikely that a court will order ABC to tear down completed construction to accommodate Peter's request for a small space even if he prevails on the merits after a full trial. Thus, Peter's injury will be irreparable if the construction is not stopped by a preliminary injunction. The remedy at law is inadequate.

Feasibility. An injunction will not issue unless the court has the ability to enforce the order. Peter will have to prove that a preliminary injunction halting construction and requiring changes in the construction in the mall to accommodate the small rental space he desires would not involve excessive supervision by the court. Courts prefer to issue prohibitory orders rather than mandatory ones. If Peter can convince the court that it could fashion an order requiring ABC to accommodate him in their new mall without requiring court supervision of construction, this element is satisfied.

Balancing of hardships. Courts will always balance the hardships when deciding whether to issue a preliminary injunction. As discussed above, if Peter is not awarded a preliminary injunction to stop construction, it will be too late to order a permanent injunction after a final decision on the merits since a court would not order the mall torn down and rebuilt to accommodate Peter's needs. On the other hand, a preliminary injunction halting construction could result in a major disruption for ABC. An interruption in construction could lead to the loss of suppliers, construction workers, and future lessees who would seek other opportunities rather than await the outcome of trial. However, since ABC never promised Peter a completion date and was constantly changing lessees and size of the space in the East Wing of the mall (first a small space to Peter, then all the space to a toy company, then divided between four or five major lessees), the court may find that the disruption is not major in view of the permanent damage Peter may suffer.

Defenses: Laches. Equitable relief, such as an injunction, is not available if the applicant for relief has unreasonably delayed the assertion of the claim and this delay prejudices the defendant. On August 1, Peter learned through a newspaper column that ABC had agreed to lease the entire East Wing, including Peter's space, to a toy company. Peter did not contact ABC until March of 1992. During this time, ABC commenced construction. A court may well deny Peter's request for a preliminary injunction because his belief that ABC would otherwise accommodate him was unreasonable when a simple phone call to assert his claim under the lease would have avoided the serious disruption in construction he is now seeking.

22. Can Peter eventually force ABC to build and lease to him a space as described in the lease agreement of July 1, 1991? Discuss.

Peter is also seeking a court order compelling ABC to lease him the space described in their original agreement. In effect, Peter is seeking specific performance of his contractual rights under the lease. In order to obtain specific performance, Peter will have to establish the following elements:

Breach of contract: Terms sufficiently definite and certain? An order of specific performance requires a finding that the defendant breached a contract containing terms that are definite and certain such that the order can be formulated. Although Peter and ABC may have agreed in principle to a lease of specified physical dimensions in the East Wing of the mall, there was no provision for when the mall would be completed. This omission can be overcome since the courts will imply a reasonable time for performance if no time is stated. Thus, a definite and certain contract existed and ABC committed a breach by anticipatory repudiation when it informed Peter in March 1992 that it would not rent any space in the mall to Peter.

Inadequate remedy at law. To obtain permanent relief through specific performance, Peter must show that money damages would be inadequate. As discussed under this element with respect to the preliminary injunction, the existence of a property interest and the difficulty of predicting lost profits (here for the entire length of the lease) make the legal remedy of damages inadequate. ABC may argue that Peter's appropriate legal remedy is the difference in rent between the ABC-Peter lease and the cost to lease comparable space elsewhere. Given the importance of location for Peter's business and the uncertainty of how a different location may affect Peter's business, this argument should not prevail.

Feasibility. Once again, if no space exists in the current construction plans, a court would have to issue an order mandating revisions in the construction plans. This may pose excessive supervision problems, which the court does not wish to undertake.

Mutuality of remedy. As long as the court can secure Peter's concomitant performance (payment of rent), this requirement is satisfied.

Defenses. Peter's failure to assert his rights in a timely fashion while ABC continued construction and made other lease arrangements will constitute laches—a bar to a specific performance award.

23. What remedies, if any, does CARS have against Brown? Discuss.

Liability theory

CARS performed $5,000 worth of work on Brown's car. The problem is that Brown did not contract with CARS for the work, Smith did. Therefore, CARS has no claim for contract damages against Brown. CARS may attempt to claim recovery on the basis of restitution, in that Brown would be unjustly enriched if he were allowed to retain the benefit of CARS's work without paying for it. Restitutionary recovery through quasi-contract is proper only when the plaintiff has conferred a benefit on the defendant with the reasonable expectation of payment. The problem is CARS had a reasonable expectation of payment from Smith, not Brown. Some courts would find that since CARS did not expect payment from Brown at the time of service, no action in quasi-contract would lie. Other courts would find the provision of the service with the expectation of payment from someone and the receipt and retention of the benefit by Brown would be a sufficient basis for recovery.

Remedy

Should recovery be allowed, it will be measured by the value of the services conferred upon Brown. The proper measure would likely be the increased value of the car attributable to CARS work because the benefit conferred was the improvement of Brown's property. This might or might not be equal to the $5,000 value of the services.

Constructive trust. Brown sold the auto repaired by CARS to Jones for $8,000. CARS may attempt to maximize its recovery by claiming this increased amount on a constructive trust theory. Under this theory, if the plaintiff can trace either property or proceeds to that which was unjustly received, the plaintiff could ask the court to impose a constructive trust upon the property or proceeds for the benefit of the plaintiff. It is highly unlikely that CARS's claim in quasi-contract would justify imposition of a constructive trust. If CARS was permitted to trace the proceeds, CARS may attempt to trace the $8,000 received by Brown to the repair of the auto by CARS. However, Brown commingled the $8,000 with $14,000 in an existing bank account. He then withdrew $20,000 and lost it all gambling, leaving $2,000 in the account. Under the lowest intermediate balance rule, CARS would be limited to a constructive trust claim on the $2,000 left in the account at most. Furthermore, CARS would have no claim to the $1,000 Brown won in the state lottery and later deposited into the account since it is not traceable to the benefit CARS conferred upon Brown.

Equitable lien. Under this theory, a plaintiff can ask the court to impose a lien on property or proceeds traceable to that which was unjustly received equal in amount to the value of that which was improperly received. However, the imposition of an equitable lien would be limited by the same equity and tracing problem discussed above in connection with constructive trust.

24. What remedies, if any, does CARS have against Jones? Discuss.

CARS has no remedy against Jones. Jones would have no liability in quasi-contract because Jones did not own the car or receive a benefit at the time CARS performed the services. Additionally, under the UCC, Jones would take the car free of any claims against it because Jones gave value and acted in good faith when buying the car.

25. Is the firm entitled to an injunction? Discuss.

In order to be entitled to an injunction, Lawyer Services, Inc., will first have to establish that either one of its two alleged tort claims have any validity.

Defamation

Defamation is a tort cause of action that alleges damage to reputation. In order to establish a prima facie case, the Lawyer Services must show that a defamatory statement was made, it was of or concerning the plaintiff, there was a publication, and that there were damages to the firm's reputation. Since this particular defamation action does not appear to be a matter of public concern, the additional factors of fault and falsity required by the First Amendment are not required.

Defamatory statement. A defamatory statement is one based on fact, not opinion, and it must either be defamatory on its face or shown to be defamatory through the use of inducement and innuendo. Here, the plaintiff carried around a sign saying that the law firm is "crooked" and that the "firm stole" her money. While "crooked" by itself would likely to be more opinion based, the fact that it was combined with the words that the firm stole her money creates a sufficient factual foundation for a defamatory statement. Since such a statement would definitely affect the law firm's reputation, the first element of the cause of action is shown.

Of or concerning plaintiff. Lawyer Services, Inc., will not have to resort to the task of "pleading colloquium" as the statement clearly referred to the firm on its face, and thus this element is satisfied.

Publication. Publication can be either intentional or negligent. Sufficient publication occurs when the defamatory statement is conveyed to someone other than the plaintiff to one who understands the defamatory comment. Here, walking up and down the street for three weeks is sufficient to meet this requirement since it was intentional and, without a doubt, someone saw the sign and understood it.

Damages to reputation. Since the "sandwich" board was written, this defamation action is based in libel. Further, because it is defamatory on its face, all jurisdictions will recognize presumed general damages of injury to reputation (i.e., minority view of libel per se and libel per quad is inapplicable). Thus, though Lawyer Services, Inc., would have to plead and prove pecuniary losses, they have a prima facie showing of defamation. (Note: Jane has no defense based on truth as the evidence shows that the doctor was paid.)

Trade libel. Trade libel is an offshoot of a defamation action and has the same essential elements for its prima facie case. There is one critical distinction between a simple defamation action and trade libel in that many jurisdictions require the plaintiff to show actual injury in order to state a cause of action. Often, this requirement is only satisfied by actual evidence of lost customers. Thus, if Lawyer Services, Inc., is in this type of jurisdiction, they will have to present such evidence in order to pursue a claim under this theory.

Injunction

Since Lawyer Services, Inc., has made out a cause of action for defamation and probably one for trade libel, the firm is entitled to an appropriate remedy.

In order to get an injunction, the plaintiff must show that the legal remedy is inadequate, that a property interest is involved, that it is feasible, balancing and that there are no defenses.

Inadequacy of the Legal Remedy. Inadequacy of the legal remedy can take many forms. Two that are very on point here are that damages are too speculative and the possibility of multiplicity of suits.

In any action for an injury to reputation, the damages are likely to be too speculative due to the nature of the injury. It is extremely difficult to put a dollar amount on reputational harm. Further, there is the probability that this former client will not desist in her activities resulting in the firm having to make continuous suits to recover damages.

The firm alleged that an injunction was necessary to protect its reputation and to stop a continuing decrease in its earnings and the number of walk-in clients. These are not adequate grounds for the granting of an injunction because they merely display a relief for damages — they do not indicate why the damages are inadequate. However, for the above reasons, the damages are inadequate.

Property Interest. At common law, injunctions were only granted when the dispute centered around personal or real property interest. Here, the injury is to reputation. Courts, however, have used two theories to get around the requirement of a property interest to allow injunctive relief in other types of harms. First, some courts just disregard the requirement altogether. Second, other more creative courts just enlarge the definition of property to include almost any kind of injury, including damages to business and reputation.

Thus, while at common law, Lawyer Services, Inc., would not meet the property requirement, in all modern jurisdictions, the harm to reputation interests alone would be sufficient "property" for an injunction to lie.

Feasibility. Feasibility is really an issue of the ability of the court to enforce the contempt power associated with an injunction. The problem is often one of supervision, and for this reason, courts prefer to state injunctions in the negative as opposed to mandatory orders to do a specific act.

Feasibility will be accomplished here merely by the court telling Jane not to picket in front of the firm.

Balance. The balancing part of the test is usually limited to nuisance and encroachment cases and in all likelihood would not be applicable in a defamation action. If a court were to apply it, it would balance the hardship to Jane versus the hardship to the firm.

Defenses

Prior restraints

With defamation actions, an injunction is usually unattainable due to the defense that an injunction is a prior restraint on free speech. The defendant's First Amendment right to free speech is greatly respected by the courts, and the United States Supreme Court has made it quite clear that a prior restraint on free speech is almost, per se, unconstitutional, requiring a very compelling state interest. Such an interest is not in existence in a factual setting between a deranged client and a local law firm.

Thus, even though Jane's attack on the law firm is apparently without basis, the firm will not be able to enjoin her on defamation grounds. A similar result occurred under substantially similar facts in one Supreme Court case.

A possibility still exists for the law firm under their trade libel theory. Assuming that they are able to state a cause of action by showing a direct loss of customers in those jurisdictions requiring it, courts are much more likely to grant an injunction over a prior restraint defense if the underlying cause of action is trade libel because the protection of such speech is not as essential as noncommercial speech.

However, it is unlikely that it would apply in this setting as Jane is not a commercial entity herself. Since injunctions are largely in the court's discretion, a court will likely distinguish this setting from one where, for example, Xerox defames IBM.

CONTRACT REMEDIES

MONEY DAMAGES – normal remedy; should place non-breaching party in position he would have been in had the contract been performed.

- **Restitution** – recovery of money already paid to breaching party (less possible *quantum meruit* offset).
- **Reliance Costs** – recovery for out-of-pocket expenses in preparing to perform.
- **Incidental Costs** – recovery of costs necessitated by breach directly relating to the contract itself (e.g., shipping, storage, inspection, reselling, or repurchasing).
- **Expected Bargained For Benefit** – ***not*** including anticipated profits (see consequential costs).
  - **SALES CONTRACTS** – difference between the market price at the time of breach and the contract price.
  - **SERVICE CONTRACT**
    - **Employee** – full contract price *if* she has performed or stands ready to do so (***less*** mitigation).
    - **Employer** – recovery limited to difference in cost to replace.
- **Consequential Damages** – money damages resulting from special situation of non-breaching party (***not*** including mental anguish or inconvenience).
  - **FORESEEABLE** – ***HADLEY v. BAXENDALE*** – reasonably foreseeable costs and losses contemplated by both parties at the time of the contract may be recovered.
  - **MITIGATION** – non-breacher's recovery must be reduced by amount yielded or yieldable by reasonable efforts to reduce costs of breach.
- **Liquidated Damages** – contractual provision setting the total amount of all money damages in the event of breach (does ***not*** bar non-monetary remedies); if invalid, non-breachor may prove and collect actual damages.
  - **REASONABLE AMOUNT** – amount must be reasonable in light of parties' contemplations at the time of contract.
  - **NECESSARY** – amount of actual damages must be difficult to ascertain.
  - **TAILORED TO CONTRACT** – provision must be tailored to nature of contract (i.e., ***not*** boilerplate).
- **Punitive Damages** – only available in extreme cases of malicious or intentional breach (that constitute a separate tort).

SPECIFIC PERFORMANCE – court may order breaching party to perform the contract.

- **Contract Must be Valid and Enforceable**
- **Money Damages Must be Inadequate**
  - **UNIQUE SUBJECT MATTER** –land, stock of close corporation, one-of-a-kind item.
  - **AMOUNT NOT ASCERTAINABLE**
- **No Special Problems of Enforcement** – (e.g., personal service contract may ***not*** be specifically enforced).
- **Subject to Equitable Defenses** – look for (1) *unclean hands*, (2) *laches*, (3) *estoppel*.

RESCISSION – cancellation of the contract to put parties as they were before the contract.

- **Grounds**
  - **MUTUAL MISTAKE IN FORMATION**
  - **FRAUD** – knowing misrepresentation of material fact relied upon by non-breachor.
  - **MAJOR BREACH CHANGING NATURE OF AGREEMENT**
- **Requirements**
  - **NON-BREACHING PARTY MUST HAVE CLEAN HANDS**
  - **NOTIFICATION WITHIN REASONABLE TIME**
  - **RESTORATION OF BREACHER TO STATUS QUO** – ***non-breachor*** must return all consideration unless alteration or change made in good faith reliance that breachor would perform.

REFORMATION – court may reform contract to accurately describe the actual agreement if there was a mutual mistake.

QUASI-CONTRACT – if no formal contract and work has been partly or fully performed, plaintiff may collect reasonable value of services; if an express contract was breached, P may sue on the contract or, if there are grounds for rescission, rescind it and sue for the reasonable value of services performed or goods transferred using the quasi-contract theory. (This is actually an alternative theory for money damages based on equity rather than contract.)

NOTES

NOTES

NOTES

NOTES

NOTES

NOTES

NOTES

NOTES

NOTES